Discourse Perspectives on Hebrew Poetry in the Scriptures

United Bible Societies Monograph Series

1. Sociolinguistics and Communication
2. The Cultural Factor in Bible Translation
3. Issues in Bible Translation
4. Bridging the Gap: African Traditional Religion and Bible Translation
5. Meaningful Translation: Its Implication for the Reader
6. The Apocrypha in Ecumenical Perspective
7. Discourse Perspectives on Hebrew Poetry in the Scriptures

UBS Monograph Series, No. 7

Discourse Perspectives on Hebrew Poetry in the Scriptures

Ernst R. Wendland, Editor

UNITED BIBLE SOCIETIES
Reading, UK
New York

UBS Monograph 7

Printed in the United States of America
ISBN 0-8267-0457-3
ABS-10/96-300-800-CM-2-104925

Contents

Foreword

A number of UBS translation consultants have been engaged for some time in the analysis of Hebrew poetry in the Scriptures from a discourse perspective. They have done this individually and in groups. This volume in the United Bible Societies' Monograph Series brings together some of the results of that study.

Anything less than the treatment of a Hebrew poetic text in its totality as a discourse is inadequate. But how to approach a poetic composition from a discourse perspective has not received much attention in the past. This study begins with the definition of a set of procedures for analyzing the discourse organization of a poetic text. Adapting these analytical guidelines would not only yield the theological and semantic content of the composition, but also its spiritual implication, emotive tones, and artistry. The chapters that follow demonstrate the application of some of these analytical procedures to a Hebrew poetic composition.

This volume is a significant contribution to the beginnings and ongoing study of a discourse analytical approach to Hebrew poetry. It is written by those who work alongside translators, and is primarily directed to those who are engaged in the difficult task of translating the Hebrew poetry of the Bible. It is, however, a useful resource also for the exegete, expositor, and student.

I wish to express my appreciation to Ernst Wendland not only for editing this volume, but also for his role as convener and coordinator of the ongoing study of this subject by a group of consultants.

Basil A. Rebera
United Bible Societies
New York
February 1994

Abbreviations

[]	Lacking in ancient texts and versions
B.C.	Before Christ
BHS	*Biblia Hebraica Stuttgartensia*
GNB	Good News Bible
HOTTP	Preliminary and Interim Report, Hebrew Old Testament Text Project
KJV	King James Version
JB	Jerusalem Bible
LXX	Septuagint
MT	Masoretic Text
NAB	New American Bible
NASB	New American Standard Bible
NEB	New English Bible
NIV	New International Version
NJB	New Jerusalem Bible
NJV	Tanakh (New Jewish Version)
NRSV	New Revised Standard Version
REB	Revised English Bible
RL	Receptor Language
RSV	Revised Standard Version
TOT	Translator's Old Testament
V	Vulgate

Books of the Bible

Gen	Genesis
Exo	Exodus
Lev	Leviticus
Deut	Deuteronomy
1,2 Sam	1,2 Samuel
1,2 Kgs	1,2 Kings
1,2 Chr	1,2 Chronicles
Psa	Psalm(s)
Pro	Proverbs
Eccl	Ecclesiastes
Isa	Isaiah
Jer	Jeremiah
Ezek	Ezekiel
Hos	Hosea

Hebrew Transliteration

The following system of transliterating Hebrew as roman script has been selected in order to accomplish two objectives: a) we wish to communicate the information to as wide an audience as possible via a relatively simple script; b) yet the authors must not be hampered by inadequate tools for communicating to the audience those details that are necessary for accomplishing the authors' purposes. The system adapted is as follows:

The English vowels, *a, e, i, o,* and *u* represent the nearest equivalent sounds of the corresponding Hebrew vowels. Gemination of consonants caused by *dagesh forte* will be represented by a single consonant, unless the study being discussed requires the distinction. The presence of *dagesh lene* will not be reflected in the representation of *gimel, daleth,* and *kaf,* since the resulting difference in English pronunciation is negligible or even nonexistent. Consonants are represented as follows:

א	'	ט	t	פּ	p
ב	v	י	y	ץ,צ	ts
בּ	b	ך,כ	k	ק	q
ג	g	ל	l	ר	r
ד	d	ם,מ	m	שׂ	s
ה	h	ן,נ	n	שׁ	sh
ו	w	ס	s	ת	th
ז	z	ע	'	תּ	t
ח	ch	ף,פ	f		

Contributors

Dr. Ernst Wendland, UBS Translation Consultant, Africa Region, based in Zambia; also Instructor, Lutheran Bible Institute and Seminary, Lusaka, Zambia.

Dr. Loren F. Bliese, UBS Translation Consultant, Africa Region, based in Addis Ababa, Ethiopia.

Dr. Robert A. Bascom, UBS Translation Consultant, Americas Region, serving in Central and South America.

Dr. Graham S. Ogden, UBS Regional Translation Coordinator, Asia-Pacific Region, based in Hong Kong.

Dr. David J. Clark, UBS Translation Consultant, Europe-Middle East Region, serving in Eastern Europe, formerly based in the Asia-Pacific Region.

Dr. William D. Reyburn, UBS Interregional Translation Consultant, based in U.S.A.

Dr. Noel D. Osborn, UBS Translation Consultant (Retired), formerly based in the Asia-Pacific Region.

The Discourse Analysis of Hebrew Poetry: A Procedural Outline

Ernst R. Wendland

Introduction

Tsaw latsaw, tsaw latsaw;
qaw laqaw, qaw laqaw;
ze'eyr sham, ze'eyr sham. (Isa 28.10)

"He is trying to teach us
letter by letter, line by line
lesson by lesson." (GNB)

Though it may be a rather free rendering of a recognized problematic passage, the Good News Bible (GNB) translation seems to capture the essence of this little poetic triplet from Isaiah. The prophet here dramatizes the mocking response of Israel's ungodly majority to his message of repentance, and, in an ironic reiteration, also to the LORD's consequent pronouncement of righteous judgment upon them (v.13).

Looking at the same verse from a literary perspective, we observe that it is a good example of the principal subject of this introductory chapter, since it so concisely illustrates many of the characteristic features of classical Hebrew poetry. Furthermore, if we lift these lines from their original context (not a recommended exegetical practice; see below) purely for the sake of their content, we discover a memorable summary of the method of discourse analysis outlined below: it should be progressive, systematic, and comprehensive. Thus any adequate study of a poetic text ought to deal with the composition in its entirety, from top to bottom of the linguistic hierarchy (or vice-versa), following an explicit plan of exposition and a holistic set of operational procedures.

The general aim of any serious text study (exegesis) is to produce a thorough analysis and explanation of the total process of message transmission as intended (presumably) by the initial author/speaker in his unique historical, cultural, and sociolinguistic environment. It involves a hypothetical reconstruction of the original performance setting, as nearly as this can be determined, in order to specify the rhetorical dynamics of the passage in terms of its formal, semantic, and pragmatic significance in relation to the primary receptor group for whom the message was composed.

As far as communicating a particular text of Scripture is concerned, the principal goal is to transmit the basic design of the discourse with respect to such interrelated features as information content, emotive expression, attitudinal tone, underlying set of values, situational relevance, and affective associations (i.e., arising from its relative degree of unity, novelty, appropriateness, impact, and appeal). The objective is to reveal as much as possible and/or practical of the essential meaning "package" conveyed during the original event of communication to receptors today who are circumstantially very remote, i.e., with regard to the temporal, geographical, ecological, social, and religious aspects of their respective life-contexts.

Careful attention must therefore be paid to all of the major components of message transmission: source, receptor, text (form, content, intent), context, and medium, in both the original and the contemporary settings. It should be noted that the medium, or channel, of communication is becoming an increasingly important consideration, as current research indicates that, not only are the Scriptures today more often heard than read, but that this oral-aural factor was also a much more important aspect of the initial process of composition and reception than has previously been recognized. Obviously it is of special relevance where poetic discourse is concerned, for as Alonso-Schökel observes, "whether it was written or not, [biblical poetry] was meant for oral recitation, in public" (Alonso-Schökel 1988:20).

In this chapter the general subject of Hebrew verse is introduced by means of an overview of how one might approach its analysis in a comprehensive and orderly way. After a brief discussion of the problematic term "poetry," an outline of ten procedural guidelines is presented which summarizes the principal steps that one is likely to follow—whether explicitly or implicitly, and in more or less detail—when examining the discourse organization of a poetic text. This may serve as a useful background to subsequent chapters where a prevailing discourse perspective both informs and unifies the methodology that is applied to varied aspects of a selection of familiar Old Testament poetic pericopes.

What is poetry?

It needs to be mentioned at the outset that the term "poetry" is itself rather misleading in the sense that it is not always possible to formally delineate in the Bible what constitutes poetic discourse and what does not (i.e., "prose"). No generic word corresponding to the English exists, only more specific subcategories, e.g., "song," "hymn," "lament," "proverb," and so forth. It is more a matter of degree than of "either-or." There are no sharply defined boundaries, only differing concentrations of linguistic features that may be evaluated in terms of their relative frequency, diversity, density, or position of occurrence on the one hand, and the nature and intensity of their rhetorical effect on the other. We thus find a variable continuum of literary types and genres that comprise the Hebrew Scriptures, ranging from those that are more to those that are less poetic in terms of a complex bundle of interrelated stylistic qualities:

POETRY <————————|————————|————————> PROSE

prosaic poetry *poetic prose*

Among the most diagnostic are the following ten formal characteristics that, due to their frequent appearance, seem to be especially representative of poetry in general and the Hebrew corpus in particular. This is especially evident when such devices occur in close conjunction with one another (*convergence*). They are arranged below in an approximate order of importance:

a) *balanced lineation*, usually exhibiting some form of *parallelism* in terms of structurally simple, coupled line-forms (especially bi- and tri-cola), which are marked by correspondences in lexical organization (e.g., gender-matching), syntax, sense, and/or sound (including a *rhythmic* system of stress accents [="meter"?]), with a major *pause point* situated at the close of each conjoined unit;

b) *pervasive repetition* of all sorts—correspondent, synonymous, and contrastive—which is often positioned in the form of *symmetrical patterns,* both linear and concentric, local and global, having an important structural function (e.g., segmentation, versification) or thematic purpose (e.g., prominence, cohesion) in the discourse;

c) a general condensation or *compaction* of linguistic structure—phonological, grammatical, and/or lexical; e.g., ellipsis (especially verb-gapping), asyndeton, morphological contraction;

d) as a specific consequence of (c), a drastic reduction in the use of the so-called Hebrew *prose particles*—the sign of the direct object (*'eth*), the definite article (*ha-*), and the relative clause marker (*'asher*);

e) unusual or *marked syntactic arrangements* of words and phrases within the line/colon/clause, including chiasmus (crossed constituents), enjambment (run-over line), and anacrusis (initial extrametrical word), as well as a deliberate *disjunction* of the elements of certain stereotyped expressions (i.e., a displacement of normally cooccuring components into both the [A] and [B] cola);

f) frequent *phonological play,* e.g., alliteration, assonance, rhyme, onomatopoeia, punning, and other sound patterns, which is employed as a means of highlighting important terms and concepts;

g) a relatively high concentration of *graphic* diction (e.g., archaic, rare, technical, proverbial, dialectal vocabulary), allusive-evocative terms, concrete *imagery,* and *figurative language* (especially metaphor and metonymy);

h) a greater incidence of other *affective* (emotive, imperative) *devices,* such as irony, allusion, rhetorical/deliberative questions, hyperbole, and intensifiers (e.g., exclamations, interjections);

i) *direct speech* as the preferred mode of composition, with associated interactive forms such as vocatives (especially the divine name) and imperatives, intended to dramatize the discourse;

j) standardized religious/liturgical or traditional *poetic forms*, such as word-pairs, introductory/concluding formulae, conventional clichés, Scriptural topics/themes/motifs—and for Hebrew also acrostic and other verbal patterns based on the alphabet.

In addition there is an approximate generic correlation which may be observed, in that texts of a more personal, expressive, and lyrical (musical) nature (i.e., where the information content is downplayed) tend to be more rhetorically marked in terms of the preceding inventory of diagnostic qualities. Thus we have the following putative progression of discourse types ranging from the least to the most poetic:

> genealogy - law - history - exposition - argument - parable - prophetic sermon - apocalypse - judgment/salvation oracle - proverb - song (e.g., penitential or panegyric psalm)

As in the case of individual lexical items, so also there are many "fuzzy borders and overlapping boundaries" (Nida forthcoming: 4) with any classification of this nature. The listing, which should not be regarded as being complete, provides merely a general guide or a rough indication of where poetry is more or less likely to be found in the Hebrew Scriptures. Another correlation that may be of greater significance is that a poetic text in the Bible is typically represented in the form of a *speech event* of some kind, one that is based upon either a real (historical) or a hypothetical interpersonal encounter involving the poet and Yahweh or his people. Accordingly it is formulated in the mode of direct discourse, often containing one or more levels of embedded quotation (cp. [i] above).

A framework for analysis

The ten procedural steps suggested below are given roughly in the order in which they would normally be applied when analyzing the compositional and stylistic features of a Hebrew poem. Although it cannot be considered more than an approximate guide, this methodology does appear to cover most of the major aspects which a thorough examination of a poetic text of Scripture ought to include—if not formally a component of the actual presentation of results, then surely as part of the essential background preparation required for any credible study of such literary discourse. Due to our distance from the original communication event and its setting, these procedures naturally can give us only a partial grasp of the form/structure, content, and function of the text as it has been received. But this is a good place to begin an investigation of the varied rhetorical purposes of the biblical poet in order to better understand, appreciate, and apply his heartfelt expression of trust, joy, praise, sorrow, anger, pain, and deepest desires—directed to a God whom he believed was both near enough to hear and powerful enough to act on behalf of his faithful people.

1. *Survey of the extralinguistic setting*

This initial stage of analysis aims to achieve a preliminary situational *contextualization*, or extralinguistic placement, of the text under consideration. This would include, in particular, its life and religious setting, or *Sitz-im-Leben*, as nearly as this can be determined by the consensus of a majority of recognized scholars in the field: biblical historians, archaeologists, anthropologists, sociologists, and literary critics. One will probably not agree with all, or even most, of the assumptions, hypotheses, and conclusions set forth in such studies, but a certain amount of useful information may be provided concerning the "who - how - when - where - and why" of the text in its original context, that is, with regard to its historical, political, sociocultural, geographical, and ecological milieu. In this connection any significant parallel or related passages (i.e., with topical, temporal, or literary connections) from the Scriptures or any other ancient texts (e.g., Akkadian, Ugaritic) ought to be studied to see what light they might shed on the general background and purpose of the passage at hand.

One must be wary, however, of certain text-critical approaches that presuppose or posit either a composite or a corrupt discourse—in other words, one that is comprised of a patchwork of disparate fragments, sources, and other forms of diverse origin—which consequently need to be clarified (or emended) by contemporary scholars. Rather, the original Hebrew (Masoretic) text ought to be assumed correct and complete as it stands, unless conclusively demonstrated otherwise, "as a check against excess" and the analyst's zeal to prove a point (Watson 1984: 17-18). It does not pay to push a historical-critical investigation of any sort too far. After all, there is so little concrete evidence available to support counter-hypotheses to a more conservative textual position, and besides, it is the final, canonical form of Scripture that must be dealt with in translation, if not interpretation as well.

But it does help exegetically in the determination of a text's author-intended meaning (in the fullest semantic and pragmatic sense) to recognize the particular genre and subtype of a given composition. One would need to know whether a given psalm, for example, was intended to "praise the LORD" or complain (lament) to him; whether it was likely to have functioned in a public liturgical setting as distinct from a private, devotional context; whether it is primarily eschatological or historical (e.g., salvation-history) in nature; or whether it is a typical wisdom piece or an imprecatory taunt (cp. #9 below). It is at this stage, once the text has been examined as fully as possible with reference to the wider purpose of composition, its initial situational setting, and the surrounding circumstances of performance, that a more discourse-oriented analytical approach may begin.

2. *Delimitation of the text*

In conjunction with a study of genre and general communicative function, an explicit delineation of the external boundaries of a poetic passage needs to be made. In other words, a text must be carefully demarcated and established with respect to its co-text as being a viable object of investigation—that is, unless an entire book is being considered. The procedures of discourse analysis cannot be regarded as valid unless they are applied to a complete, self-contained unit, or pericope, of some kind. The text must have recognizable borders that can be precisely defined and defended—at whatever level in the compositional hierarchy it happens to lie. Furthermore, a smaller segment will have to be related to the larger portion in which it is included as an integral unit, while a larger section must be broken down during the course of analysis into its constituent elements. This implies that a holistic (whole-part), *discourse perspective* has to be adopted from the start and consistently maintained throughout a particular study.

Text delimitation does not pose much of a problem in cases where long-established and universally recognized units are concerned (e.g., the individual psalms) or where poetic passages are set within an enveloping narrative account (e.g., Exo 15). Difficulties increase considerably, however, in the so-called prophetical books, especially in determining the respective boundaries and interrelationships which connect the constituent segments that comprise a sequence of oracles, for example, or a series of visions. There are a number of helps that may be utilized in this process of partitioning a textual composite, that is, in addition to one's own initial examination of the pericope in question in a reliable edition of the original: critical commentaries, study Bibles, and other translated versions, particularly those that pay serious attention to the larger discourse structure of the Scriptures (e.g., GNB, New International Version [NIV], NET).

It is important to remember that the standard chapter and verse divisions are only an approximate guide to a text's macro- and micro-organization. In certain cases they are misleading or even in obvious error, with respect to the individual verse breaks as well as seemingly complete compositions. Within the Book of Psalms, too, there are a number of questionable instances of separating what originally perhaps belonged together. The clearest example of this involves Psalms 42 and 43, which are structurally and thematically interlocked with each other as a single prayer of lament to the LORD (Psa 42.8; for another possible pairing, see Psa 9–10).

3. *Textual criticism and translation*

Once a particular poetic composition has been demarcated, at least provisionally subject to a thorough discourse analysis, it is necessary to examine the quality or physical state of the text itself. One should first consult the critical apparatus of the original as well as any textual commentary or specific study which deals with this subject; e.g., reports of the Hebrew Old Testament Text Project or works such as Barr (1968), Würthwein (1979), and McCarter (1986). Modern translations into English, French, Spanish, etc. make occasional reference to the major variant readings in footnotes, thus alerting the analyst to possible problem areas that need to be further investigated.

Poetry often presents additional difficulties pertaining to the original text because of its special literary features as listed earlier, especially with regard to its common use of highly specific, rare, and/or archaic vocabulary. As already suggested, the most reliable policy to follow is the conservative one of allowing the received Hebrew (or Aramaic) text to stand without emendation if at all possible. This is certainly true in passages where the alternatives are either contradictory or not strongly supported, and otherwise, where textual corruption is likely, alterations would normally be allowed only in cases where vowel pointing or consonant segmentation is involved. Recently McCreesh has adduced evidence of a phonological nature in support of such an approach (McCreesh 1991: 13-14). Explanatory notes should be made (for possible future reference) in order to provide the reasoning behind and evidence for any deviations from the standard Masoretic text that have been adopted in one's analysis.

Once the original setting has been studied and the text itself specified, it is time to prepare one's own translation from the Hebrew. Ideally, for comparative purposes, a dynamic, functionally equivalent version as well as a more literal rendering ought to be made. It should be a complete job, from beginning to end of the pericope under study. A helpful way of preparing oneself for this task is to read the poem through several times, aloud and in the original, both to get a feel for the whole and also to note any significant phonological features that occur along the way. Special attention needs to be given to problem passages, whether the difficulty concerns form, content, or both, for these areas may hold the key for interpreting a larger pattern or plan within the whole (and vice-versa). The same applies to verses that are at least initially ambiguous, that is, the grammar or lexis allows two or more different interpretations, either complementary or contrastive in nature. The analyst may later discover that one or another of these alternatives is firmly supported by either the immediate or the wider discourse structure of the pericope.

To some, this sort of translational exercise might seem like a waste of time, since there are so many versions and commentaries available to which one could refer in order to derive an exegetical understanding of a poem's microstructure. That may be true, but the discipline of putting everything together in the process of coming to one's own decisions about *what* the poet was trying to say—and *how*—is the best way of getting ready for a comprehensive discourse study. In fact, this is the only means of really familiarizing oneself with the text as an act of communication within a specific literary, theological, and sociocultural setting. One needs to experience the poetry firsthand and close-up—sensorially as well as cognitively and emotively—before one attempts to analyze it in terms of its broader structures, themes, and purposes.

4. *Spatialization of the text*

This is a step which may be carried out while doing the text-critical work and translation (cp. #3 above), though it may be preferable to do it separately in the original language, so that the text's phonological and morphological features are also revealed. The exercise consists of a positional vertical (*paradigmatic*) and horizontal (*syntagmatic*) display of the discourse on a clause-by-clause basis, as each occurs in sequential order and according to the natural arrangement of syntactic units, as follows:

LINK // PRE-VERB1 // P-V2 // *VERB* // POST-VERB1 // P-V2 // OTHER

The different elements that are manifested in a given clause (kernel, colon, proposition) are thus written in columns down the page where they appear in relation to the nuclear verb, whether finite or nonfinite, and made explicit if necessary. This is because in Hebrew (as well as Greek) the preverbal position is likely to be foregrounded or emphasized in some way. The chart also makes it easier to discover the patterns of repetition that constitute the basis of biblical rhetoric, whether on the micro- or macro-structure of discourse, in poetry as well as prose. Such correspondences and contrasts should be marked right on the spatialized display, for example, by using colored marking pens, so that the larger compositional schemata become apparent and can be more readily compared.

Different frequency and distribution studies may then be carried out on the basis of a selective concordance, made as the need arises, perhaps in response to any special features observed during the translation process. One might examine such items as the nature of interclausal linkage (semantic relationships), the various pre- and post-verbal constituents, verb tense sequence, nominal clauses, phonological devices (similarities and contrasts), morphologically important affixes, key terms, lexical pairs, repeated words in parallel, and so forth. Such occurrences should be recorded, tabulated, and (if accuracy and precision demand it) statistically computed with respect to number, position, and collocation. All potentially significant results may be noted for future reference as the analysis proceeds. Again, it is important to look for any strong correspondences, tendencies, and patterns which are manifested by the data—or the opposite phenomena, i.e., unexpected inconsistencies, novelties, and/or interruptions in a prevailing sequence or established arrangement of verbal elements.

5. Text segmentation

A provisional segmentation of a poetic composition can be made on the basis of a number of features of the text as previously analyzed, including its traditional division into "open" and "closed" paragraphs, i.e., *pethucha* and *sethuma* (Würthwein 1979: 21). But the primary indicator of structural organization in poetry is lexical repetition as manifested especially in *parallelism*. Patterns of *contiguous* (or internal) parallelism serve to establish the smallest intrinsic segment of discourse, namely, the poetic line or utterance unit (colon, stich). A colon averages three rhythmic words or accent-units, each one containing a single major stress. The range is from one to six words per colon. These cola regularly occur in conjoined pairs that together comprise a complete semantic-syntactic constituent or verse. About 75% of all poetic verses in the Hebrew Bible consist of bicola, versus roughly 20% for three-lined tricola, and less than 5% for monocola and multicola (Korpel and de Moor 1988: 15). The Masoretic accentual system provides a fairly reliable indication of these basic divisions, but it needs to be substantiated and occasionally corrected by means of the principal rhetorical and structural features of the text.

Insufficient attention has heretofore been given to the phenomenon of *noncontiguous* repetition, other than that involving exact restatement, namely, the periodic refrains that segment certain Psalms (e.g., 42–43, 46, 49, 56, 57, and 59; cp. Raabe 1990). This oversight concerns not only obvious lineal (i.e., external) parallelism, but it also applies to other less complete types of phonological, syntactic, lexical, and semantic recursion. Not many of these separated but related utterances manifest the same degree of parallelism as that found in adjacent cola. Nevertheless the reiteration of form and content is often significant, for it serves a crucial structural function by helping to demarcate the individual segments that make up a larger poetic arrangement, hence also to format the composition as a whole (cp. Wendland 1988). An initial indication of how the text is arranged according to these larger patterns of lexical-semantic recycling may be derived from the preceding stage of analysis (i.e., *spatialization,* step 4).

The key feature to observe here is the discourse position of the parallel utterances in relation to one another. The focal recursion, whether analogous, antithetical, or consequential in nature, may appear at the respective beginnings of two or more discrete poetic units, either at the same or at difference levels of the organizational hierarchy. This may be termed *anaphora,* for the sake of abbreviated reference. A similar type of marking may occur at the respective endings of corresponding segments (i.e., *epiphora*). Alternatively, the reiteration may be found at the beginning and ending of the same larger compositional unit (*inclusio*); at the conclusion of one unit and the opening of the next in an overlapping ("hinged") type of construction (*anadiplosis*); or less frequently, at the close of one segment and the onset of a subsequent but removed unit, thus distinguishing an integral section in between (*exclusio*).

One other common type of recursion needs to be mentioned to complete the basic structural inventory, namely, that of a *concentric* nature, i.e., a *ring* (three constituents), *chiasmus* (four constituents), or *introversion* (more than four constituents). In such cases an important topical element (key word[s], phrase, colon) is frequently located in the center of two or more pairs of corresponding enclosing units, thus highlighting the thematic peak, emotive climax, and/or structural turning point of the entire discourse.

In short, patterns of significant repetition normally criss-cross a typical poetic text in the Hebrew Scriptures, not in random fashion, but in a way which manifests—both to the eye and also to the ear—how the composition is organized formally as well as thematically. Due to its functional importance in the discourse, such architectonic recursion is usually supplemented by other literary devices that are used to reinforce this essential oral-aural "typesetting" process.

6. Confirmation of the textual organization

Once the discourse has been provisionally demarcated by means of repetition, both local and global, it is necessary to verify the poetic structure that emerges by means of a closer analysis of the text. In addition to repetition, other rhetorical devices need to be examined in context to see whether, taken together, they confirm or disprove the boundaries initially established. These features operate in concert to perform two major functions in the discourse, namely, disjunction and conjunction. The result is a unified composition that nevertheless manifests a diverse range of centrifugal (loosening) and centripetal (tightening) structural forces, whether extensive or limited in scope, yet all in dynamic tension with one another as they highlight either the whole or its constituent parts (cp. Grossberg 1989).

Disjunctive devices help to mark a break or border in the text—a point of discontinuity. When considered together with the various hierarchical patterns of repetition mentioned above, these formal and semantic features provide additional evidence for or against a particular segmentation of the discourse. Among the more important of such *bounding* markers in Hebrew poetry are: sudden shifts in mood, mode (i.e., direct/indirect speech), meter, point-of-view, person, speaker, addressee, topic, time, and deixis (or location); formulaic utterances ("So speaks the LORD . . ," "And it will be . . . ," "Hear the word of the LORD . . ," etc.); exclamatory expressions, including intensifiers (e.g., "surely"), vocatives, imperatives, verbless predication, and frequently graphic imagery, especially metaphor and metonymy; explicit mention of the name of God, notably in compound phrases with attributive praise epithets; asyndeton (absence of explicit conjunction between utterances); chiasmus—the more elaborate it is, the more diagnostic as a structural signal—and other unusual alterations in word order, either front-shift or, less commonly, back-shift; condensation, as realized in particular by a short, emphatic monocolon; or expansion, e.g., a tricolon.

These markers operate at different levels in the discourse hierarchy and the governing poetic arrangement, either at the beginning or at the ending of a particular unit, to distinguish *aperture* and *closure* respectively. Some have a preference for one position or the other, e.g., a vocative at the onset or an emphatic monocolon at the close of a segment. But each poetic discourse must be analyzed on its own terms and with respect to the principal rhetorical strategy that is developed within it, in keeping with the poet's central theme and communicative purpose. Any point in a poem which manifests a special concentration, or *convergence*, of such features is bound to be significant with regard to the structure, content, and/or function of the composition in its totality.

A diversity of *conjunctive* devices serve to mark continuity and progression within a text, that is, to *bond* the various segments together into a unified whole (cp. Hagstrom 1988). They, too, may be of a formal or a semantic nature to effect *cohesion* and/or *coherence*, which are the principal types of connectivity within verbal discourse. The repetition of different linguistic features is again crucial in the establishment of formal connectivity within a given segment, at whatever level in the overall structural organization this happens to be. There may be a reiteration of sounds, morphological markers, lexical expressions, rhythmic units (accent lines), parallel forms, link words, and syntactic constructions (the last two items mentioned may, of course, create a juncture without repetition).

Coherence may be of a topical or a logical nature. The selection of meanings from within a certain semantic field or referential domain establishes a network of significance that contributes greatly to the unity of subject or theme. A logical development may take various courses, depending on the genre of poetry concerned, e.g., a prophetic judgment oracle: revelation of sin(s) → accusation of the guilty → pronouncement of judgment → specification of punishment; a lyric hymn: invocation to worship → exposition of Yahweh's mighty works of deliverance → words of praise → dedication to God's service. Such generic sequences may be verbally specified in further detail according to the nature of the discourse being analyzed.

Finally, it is time to put it all together (*synthesis*, cp. Watson 1984: 20) in a further revision of the poetic text's presumed organization—its principal points of disjunction, stretches of conjunction, and patterns of recursion as they operate in interaction to establish the larger framework of discourse design. There should be a substantial matching of results or else something is wrong. In other words, the areas of closure and aperture on different structural strata ought to coincide; the progressive unfolding of a particular topic should fall within the boundaries of some recognizable segment; and smaller units combine inclusively to form larger ones. Such literary patterns and frames tend to be harmonious but never perfect, and the data must not be skewed or idiosyncratically interpreted in order to make elements fit into some preconceived scheme. The principal criterion is that of overall meaning; while poets may deliberately skew textual form for special effect, they do not often consciously introduce semantic confusion to complicate their intended message. Variety and novelty in usage are always carefully balanced by the regularity imposed by the religious tradition.

The procedures of analysis thus involve an on-going *inductive* process whereby one goes back and forth over the different structural divisions as they are revealed, as well as up and down the text's compositional hierarchy. It is necessary to take into consideration the broader criteria of poetic form, thematic content, and rhetorical intent both individually and together as they are realized by various specific stylistic features exemplifying either consonance or dissonance. In the end a more or less concrete realization of the literary-linguistic structure can be postulated, from the *verse* (bi-/tri-/tetra-colon), to the *strophe* (several related verses), to the *stanza* (several related strophes), and on up the ladder of inclusion to encompass the poem as a complete whole (e.g., *canticle, oracle*). It is an artistic as well as theological discourse and hence one whose communicative significance in terms of function is greater, and perhaps different from, either the sum, the sequence, or any selection of its individual parts.

7. *Location of points of prominence*

The patterns constituted by formal recursion (discovered in step #5) in conjunction with the several literary devices mentioned above (#6) may also be utilized by the poet to highlight distinct points of prominence within the text. Frequently this occurs at the central core of an included structural unit (strophe, stanza), at the midpoint of the entire composition, or at their respective external boundaries, particularly the last. An extensive or unfolding construction, such as a parallel series or a chiastic introversion, effects a progressive *foregrounding*, whereby the central and/or final element in the series realizes the peak (thematic focus) or climax (emotive high) of a given segment. A concentrated co-occurrence of rhetorical features constitutes *emphasis*, which is usually more local in scope and related in form to other points in the overall structure of a section.

Such areas of poetic intensity in biblical discourse serve to attract the reader/listener's attention—not simply for their own sake (i.e., a purely artistic function), but in order to stress some important aspect of a text's wider meaning. The latter refers to its essential theological message and/or functional purpose as related both to the original situational or sociological setting and also to the poet's communicative aim(s). These diverse features normally coexist in dynamic tension and reflect off of one another to reinforce the associative semantic aspects of any verbal art form, that is, its significance with regard to relevance, import, novelty, forcefulness, evocative-emotive power, and aesthetic appeal (beauty).

8. Formulation of a thematic/semantic summary

Once the larger organizational structure of a poetic piece has been fairly well-established and its individual points of prominence identified, it is often useful to summarize the results by constructing a thematic and/or semantic outline of the whole. With respect to a *thematic* overview, an evaluation of the relevance or importance of any item considered for inclusion is normally determined on the basis of a comparative, synchronic and diachronic *key-term analysis*. This may be done according to the criteria of *quantity*, i.e., the diversity and distribution of items included under a given topic, motif, or focal word, and *quality*, i.e., the significance of the material in relation to the text's overall architectural design, theme, and purpose. This synopsis should be guided—insofar as this is possible by a distant, outside observer—by the formal structural markers previously located inductively within the discourse itself (i.e., emically; cf. #5-6), and not on some neat, but artificial, logical or theological etic formulation.

A more detailed and theoretically precise *semantic* résumé of a poetic work may also be prepared if necessary. The traditional classification according to three types of parallelism—synonymous, antithetic, and synthetic—has tended to obscure the fact that a more diverse set of syntagmatic relations links the elements of colon couplets and clusters in the text, and hence much more precise designations are possible, even necessary, for analysis. Thus, like any other discourse (e.g., narrative, exposition, argument), a poem may be analyzed, and then synthesized again, in terms of its sequential interpropositional connections to form a hierarchical network that encompasses the entire composition.

On the generic level one may apply the three universal organizing principles of class, time, and space along with their respective derivatives: rank, consequence, and dialogic alternation (Nida forthcoming: 5). These broad categories may be further specified in terms of a relatively fixed set of semantic/logical classes, e.g., CONSEQUENCE: cause-effect, reason-result, means-purpose, condition-consequence, concession-contraexpectation, grounds-implication [i.e., praise, petition, or profession] (cp. Beekman, Callow, and Kopesec 1981; Nida 1975: chapter 5). The entire structure of a given text may thus be displayed in the form of a comprehensive tree diagram (see the example of Psa 30 in chapter 2). It is important to remember, however, that a strictly binary and/or polar segmentation of the discourse may be misleading if considered in isolation, because the individual cola (propositions), along with their various (sub)groupings, often forge additional meaningful relations with other textual constituents, either on the same or some different level of structural organization.

It should also be kept in mind that the explicit delineation of a poem's larger framework, whether formulated according to major theme and subthemes or its semantic-logical structure, represents but a partial explication of its meaning, namely, that of a cognitive, conceptual nature. This aspect may, in fact, be only a relatively minor component of the poem's total communicative aim and effect, that is, in comparison with its associated connotative significance and rhetorical dynamics (see #9 below).

9. Interactional analysis in terms of speech event/acts

This analytical procedure is an extension of the initial investigation carried out during a study of the extratextual setting (cp. #1). Here one wishes to take a closer look at how the text probably functioned both internally and externally as it was developed during performance (proclamation/recital/song), which, in the case of a liturgical piece like a psalm, would have certainly been repeated on a regular basis, either publicly or in private. First of all, how do the central participants *within* the discourse relate to one another in terms of their various roles and key communicative intentions as the drama of personal interaction unfolds, namely, the psalmist/prophet (protagonist), his "enemies"/a hostile audience (antagonists), and God (the supreme arbiter)? And secondly, on the larger compositional level of message transmission, what was the author seeking to *do* through his poem—how did he intend the message to *affect* his receptors—what *impact* did he want his carefully selected "modes of discourse" to have upon them, e.g., narration, reflection, invocation, interrogation, rebuke, warning (Collins 1987:42-43)? In this connection one could also analyze the text in terms of its principal sociological functions, namely, the "interpersonal, imperative, informative, emotive, performative, and aesthetic" impulses (Nida and de Waard 1986: 25-31).

Obviously it is not possible to be dogmatic or prescriptive about such a study, since we are so far removed from the original event in terms of history, culture, environment, and world view. There are, in fact, several distinct stages of possible contextual focus in between the initial and current contemporary settings, e.g.: *consolidation* as the text was subsequently being circulated and transmitted via either oral or written tradition; *canonization*, after a given text was officially accepted as being a part of the received corpus of Scripture; and *concretization*, when in the passing of time the literal text tended to become fixed hermeneutically and was transformed (for many) into a verbal icon, an object of human reverence rather than a source of divine revelation.

Despite the uncertainties involved, it is useful to make a reasoned hypothesis concerning the poem's chief internal (embedded) and external communicative objectives, implications, and consequences, since all such pragmatic aspects of meaning were integral constituents of the message when it was first composed and then conveyed to its receptors. For example, what were the primary functional motivations that the poet wished to realize in his audience by means of his work in keeping with the cognitive-emotive principle of *relevance*? In other words, what was the overall impact of the message in terms of effectiveness and efficiency, that is, the level of *contextual effects* stimulated in relation to degree of *processing effort* expended on the part of readers/hearers (Gutt 1991: 30; Hatim and Mason 1991: 93-94)? This complex interpersonal factor must be given due consideration during analysis, especially if one intends to produce a dynamically-equivalent translation for people today who are inevitably living under very different situational (including media-age), social, and spiritual circumstances, and whose interpretation is influenced by a cognitive environment that may vary greatly from that of original receptors.

The fabric of literary discourse thus includes another crucial strand, one which encompasses a hierarchy that will correspond in broad outline with its previously determined structural-thematic framework. Every distinct formal unit of the text—from the line/colon to the composition as a whole—may be viewed as manifesting a particular function, or functional complex, in relation to its audience then and now. As literary analysts such as Kugel (1981: 8) and Alter (1985: 29) have pointed out, this feature is especially prominent in Hebrew poetry by virtue of its characteristic development by means of coupled, or parallel, lines. Thus colon B typically manifests some manner of addition or heightening with respect to colon A in terms of semantic and/or pragmatic qualities such as elaboration (expansion), intensification, specification, figuration, emotive expression, dramatization (direct speech), and so forth. All of these special effects need to be examined in relation to one another, both sequentially and also from the perspective of the composition considered as a whole.

This *interactional structure,* to give it a name, unites the original and all subsequent receptor groups with the original author/poet through his verbal discourse with respect to a specific sociological setting and cultural-religious context on the one hand, and a world- or life-view (whether shared or disparate) on the other. The dynamics of such an interpersonal engagement via a theologically-oriented message may be described and evaluated in terms of the standard distinctions made within the framework of *speech-act* theory, namely: the *locution* (the formal realization of a given segment of text, including its poetic-rhetorical devices); *illocution* (the goal or aim of any locution); and the *perlocution* (what it actually accomplished with regard to receptor behavior—cognition, emotion, or volition). The actual consequences of verbal communication of an artistic nature, of course, are not usually specified in the biblical record. Attention is therefore focussed upon the assumed illocutionary intent of individual and conjoined segments in the sequence of cola, verses, strophes, stanzas, and indeed the poem as a whole, i.e., the "text act" (Hatim and Mason 1991: 91).

What lends credence to these assumptions concerning the interactional structure? The principal source of evidence must always be the text itself—not some hypothetical reconstruction of its presumed context. Explicit and implicit clues within the discourse will normally alert the investigator to covert presuppositions and implicatures as well as to motives that are fairly apparent. One would note, for example, the presence of verbs selected from the topical field of worship and praise (to God) as opposed to accusation and condemnation (of the ungodly); the attitudinal stance conveyed by such devices as rhetorical questions, irony, hyperbole, paradox, personification, and exclamatory utterances; the emotive tone evoked by vocatives, intensifiers, familiar theological motifs and symbols, or conventional (sometimes also controversial) religious concepts; and the semantic or pragmatic relationships that exist between designated propositions (cola), whether contiguous (syntagmatic connection) or removed (paradigmatic association) (cp. Wendland 1991).

All of these and similar features must be considered both individually and in rhetorical relation to one another within the previously established structural-thematic framework when positing the most likely performance scenario or context of transmission. As far as the Book of Psalms is concerned, this hypothetical setting is not fixed but will generally fluctuate between the two functional poles of *lament* (complaint, supplication) and *eulogy* (praise, thanksgiving). The goal then is to specify, as nearly as possible, how the biblical poet sought to move his audience through the verbal artistry of his text to experience either a conversion or a confirmation with regard to their thinking and behavior concerning Yahweh—their sovereign Lord, covenant Provider, and gracious Liberator.

10. Comparison and contextualization

The last step in the analytical process builds on the preceding (#9) to conduct a more detailed elaboration of the initial stage of study (steps #1-2). It thus involves further textual and extratextual comparison as a final check on the methodology as a whole. One might begin by reexamining the poetic segment under consideration with respect to its *intra-* and *inter-textual* context, that is, "replacing" it within its original literary and theological setting. How does it relate to the next larger discourse unit in which it occurs (e.g., chapter, section) and the complete composition in terms of formal features, content (general theme with included topics), and purpose? In other words, how does it modify or elaborate upon the main idea(s) being put forward by the poet, how does it advance his argument or further express his (or Yahweh's) attitude and evaluation; how is the wider interactional structure developed or modified by this particular section; and how do the specific literary forms used here compare with those that are manifested in other portions of the same work? Similarities are important, but one would be particularly interested in the intratextual differences and what a possible explanation for these might be. The use of different translations in various languages (if possible) is a valuable aid in such a comparative exercise.

Even seemingly independent poems may have a definite reason for their position within a larger corpus; for example, the first and second psalms, which surely need to be considered together as an introduction to the Book of Psalms as a whole (Miller 1986:87). What are the implications of a given prayer-song's location for someone reading or hearing the larger whole in sequential order—or for one who is familiar with the whole and is now trying to decide how the portion at hand happens to fit in? The collection known as the "Songs of Ascents" (Psa 120–134), for example, is unified both formally and thematically (Grossberg 1989:chapter 1), and this fact must have a bearing on the interpretation of any single instance, which cannot be considered in isolation. As a case in point, Patrick Miller effectively calls attention to the various ties that link Psalm 127 with 128 and "thus press the reader to hear the two psalms in relation to each other" (1986:136).

Similar questions concerning a given poetic pericope may be addressed with respect to similar or related texts (e.g., historically, stylistically, topically) that occur elsewhere in the Bible. How are they alike and in what ways are they different in the key dimensions of form, content, and/or function? What is the possible significance of any noteworthy features of either a corresponding or a contrasting nature? How may these works have influenced one another in the history of textual composition and transmission (i.e. *intertextuality*) within the framework of the Hebrew Testament and related religious literature, e.g., the Midrash and the Mishnah? Then, for the ultimate bird's eye view: what hermeneutical and theological processes are at work in the appropriation of poetic passages from the Hebrew Scriptures (or the

Septuagint!) by the writers of the New Testament, whether through exact citation, reformulation, or allusion?

And finally, having hypothesized about the various interrelationships that a given discourse may have with its textual context, both immediate and remote, in its original setting, one should also conduct a similar study with reference to crucial *extratextual* factors pertaining to the *contemporary* receptor constituency. In short, does a translated text communicate differently today than it did then in the language and mode (e.g., poetry) of composition, and in what respects? Furthermore, what effect does the chosen medium of transmission have upon one's understanding of and appreciation for a biblical document or passage, and what effect might a shift in the channel have on people (i.e., from the written-visual to the oral-aural or audio-video modes)? Which contemporary versions seek to achieve a degree of functional equivalence (as nearly as we can determine this) by means of a poetic rendering in the receptor language? To what extent have any of these succeeded, and what are the exegetical implications of this? Which aspects of the source message get lost in either a dynamic or a literal version, and what are the consequences in terms of communicative efficiency and effectiveness? To what degree is the typographical format a factor in the process of message transmission in a modern setting?

A complete understanding, let alone total transfer, of the dynamics of each and every significant dimension of biblical literature is an obvious impossibility, especially where poetry is concerned. A thorough discourse analysis is therefore essential in order to reduce the magnitude of the failure that exegetes, translators, and Bible expositors alike, no matter how skilled, inevitably experience in this regard. Furthermore, such study enables these experts to evaluate their priorities and to gauge the degree of success which they are likely to achieve in their respective endeavors. Discourse analysis also helps them to propose various ways and means of compensating for the unavoidable skewing and loss of meaning that occurs in transmission—either translationally, within the text, or extratextually in the form of some supplementary aid, e.g., section heading, cross reference, illustration, chart, map, glossary entry, or footnote. To the latter body of recognized devices, we might add the new dimensions of interpretation made possible by more extensive explanatory/descriptive notes (as in a study Bible) or through the creative use of graphic design (typography and format) in publishing. The aim is to achieve a more accurate, appropriate, and acceptable degree of communication in relation to the particular receptor group for whom the poetic message is intended.

Some implications of a discourse-oriented analytical methodology

The ten procedural steps outlined above are an attempt to specify at least part of what goes on when we analyze a poetic composition in terms of its overall discourse construction—formal, semantic, and rhetorical (or pragmatic). These procedures are based on a standard model of communication (i.e., S—M—>R, etc.), but one which has been extended in its explanatory capacity by some important insights derived from structural semiotics, sociolinguistics, and speech-act theory. The three main components of discourse meaning are thus progressively weighted as follows:

[FORM < CONTENT < INTENT]

(< = in service of what follows/is less important than what follows)

That is to say, the particular function, or functional complex, of a poetic text in relation to its ancient as well as its current receptors is of utmost importance during analysis, whether for exegetical, expository, homiletical, or translational purposes. This is not to say that the propositional (cognitive) content of the discourse, or its distinctive stylistic (literary/linguistic) characteristics is unimportant, for an accurate understanding of these aspects of the composition must be gained before a valid description of communicative intention can be arrived at. But of paramount concern is the overall impact of the text today in terms of its effectiveness in positively reinforcing or modifying the cognitive, emotive, and volitional mind-set of receptors (and, in turn, their behavior as well) along the lines both explicitly and implicitly established by the original composition in its own setting of proclamation. This essentially spiritual process of regeneration, liberation, correction, and edification is of course completely dependent upon the enabling power of the Spirit of God (Psa 51.11; 106.33; 139.7; 143.10).

The heuristic approach implicit in the preceding notes, when fully developed and exemplified in practice, is intended to be one that is *multifaceted* (all relevant features of the discourse are considered), *eclectic* (various techniques are employed), *integrative* (an attempt is made to weave the different facets of analysis into a holistic procedure), and primarily *inductive* (it begins with and is guided by the text itself). The program is not exclusive, therefore, but is inclusive of other methodologies that focus upon one or more of the outstanding individual features of poetic discourse, e.g., phonology (McCreesh), parallelism (Kugel and Berlin), literary devices (Alter and Fisch), syntax (O'Conner and Collins), neo-rhetorical approaches (various essays in Clines et al. and Follis). The aim of the present survey was to provide a general theoretical and practical framework within which one might situate and relate these and other contemporary perspectives (see bibliography).

The point is that no single methodology is able to give us an adequate understanding of either an individual poem or a larger collection of them. Rather, one perspective needs to be complemented by another as necessary (and available) in order to cover as many as possible of the many significant aspects, dimensions, implications, and applications of biblical poetry (in the wider sense of the term). And even then our comprehension and reproduction of the whole will only be partial, a pale reflection of the original, but one which nevertheless continues to give lyric voice to the faithful people of God in personal and corporate interaction with their almighty but merciful Creator, Sustainer, Savior, and Friend.

Each of the following chapters of this monograph presents a particular application of one or more of the discourse analysis procedures outlined above in relation to a specific poetic text of the Hebrew Scriptures. A diversity of aims and methodologies is represented and illustrated in relation to a variety of pericopes. We begin with my own investigation of some prominent aspects of the compositional operations of *continuity* and *discontinuity* as manifested in the structure and setting of Psalm 30. This is followed by Loren Bliese's detailed exemplification of *symmetry and prominence* in the Book of Hosea, based on the technique of *metrical chiasmus*. Robert Bascom demonstrates the importance of including a consideration of Hebrew poetic principles when dealing with issues of a text-critical nature, with particular reference to the Song of Songs. Graham Ogden draws attention to a number of the important thematic and structural relationships between prose and poetry as they interact in a narrative text, namely, Judges 4 and 5. Isaiah's "Song of the

Vineyard" (5.1-7) is the object of David Clark's study of the significance of genre expectations in the interpretation of a poem and in its communication to a contemporary audience via translation. The practical implications of poetic discourse structure for Bible translation are also discussed in the final two contributions. William Reyburn illustrates this in his exploration of the anatomy of the acrostic lament found in Lamentations 1, while Noel Osborn carries out a similar objectives in his rhetorical analysis of Moses's "Song of the Sea" (Exo 15).

The passage which began this chapter (Isa 28.10) may well be an accurate reflection of the initial attitude that many contemporary readers and hearers of the Bible have concerning its many poetic portions. Our hope is that after studying the collection of essays contained in this modest volume, one might come to a much more positive evaluation of the Hebrew poets—one that corresponds more closely with the intention expressed by one of the lyric members of Korah's clan:

> *Beautiful words fill my mind,*
> *as I compose this song for the king.*
> *Like the pen of a [skilled] writer*
> *my tongue is ready with a poem.* (Psa 45.1; GNB, modified)

References

Alonso-Schökel, Luis. 1988. *A Manual of Hebrew Poetics*. Rome: Editrice Pontificio Instituto Biblico.

Alter, Robert. 1985. *The Art of Biblical Poetry*. New York: Basic Books.

Barr, James. 1968. *Comparative Philology and the Text of the Old Testament*. Oxford: University Press.

Beekman, John; John Callow; and Michael Kopesec. 1981. "The Semantic Structure of Written Communication." Prepublication draft (5th ed.). Dallas: Summer Institute of Linguistics.

Berlin, Adele. 1985. *The Dynamics of Biblical Parallelism*. Bloomington: Indiana University Press.

Clines, David; David Gunn; and Alan Hauser, editors. 1982. *Art and Meaning: Rhetoric in Biblical Literature*. Sheffield: JSOT Press.

Collins, Terrence. 1987. "Decoding the Psalms: A Structural Approach to the Psalter." JSOT 37. pp. 41-60.

———. 1978. *Line-Forms in Hebrew Poetry*. Rome: Biblical Institute Press.

Fisch, Harold. 1988. *Poetry with a Purpose: Biblical Poetics and Interpretation*. Bloomington: Indiana University Press.

Follis, Elaine, editor. 1987. *Directions in Biblical Hebrew Poetry*. Sheffield: JSOT Press.

Geller, Stephen. 1979. *Parallelism in Early Biblical Poetry* (Harvard Semitic Monographs 20). Missoula, MT: Scholars Press.

Grossberg, Daniel. 1989. *Centripetal and Centrifugal Structures in Biblical Poetry*. Atlanta: Scholars Press.

Gutt. Ernst-August. 1991. *Translation and Relevance: Cognition and Context*. Oxford: Basil Blackwell.

Hagstrom, David. 1988. *The Coherence of the Book of Micah* (SBL Dissertation Series 89). Atlanta: Scholars Press.

Hatim, Basil, and Ian Mason. 1991. *Discourse and the Translator*. New York: Longman.

Kugel, James. 1981. *The Idea of Biblical Poetry: Parallelism and Its History*. New Haven: Yale University Press.

McCarter, P. Kyle, Jr. 1986. *Textual Criticism: Recovering the Text of the Hebrew Bible*. Philadelphia: Fortress.

McCreesh, Thomas. 1991. *Biblical Sound and Sense: Poetic Sound Patterns in Proverbs 10-29*. Sheffield: JSOT Press.

van der Meer, Willem, and Johannes de Moor. 1988. *The Structural Analysis of Biblical and Canaanite Poetry*. Sheffield: JSOT Press.

Miller, Patrick D., Jr. 1986. *Interpreting the Psalms*. Philadelphia: Fortress Press.

Nida, Eugene A. (Forthcoming) "Translation: Possible *and* Impossible." Manuscript, pp. 1-13.

———. 1975. *Exploring Semantic Structures*. Munich: Wilhem Fink Verlag.

———, and Jan de Waard. (1986) *From One Language to Another: Functional Equivalence in Bible Translating*. Nashville: Thomas Nelson.

O'Conner, M. 1980. *Hebrew Verse Structure*. Winona Lake, IN: Eisenbrauns.

Raabe Paul. 1990. *Psalm Structures: A Study of Psalms with Refrains*. Sheffield: JSOT Press.

Watson, Wilfred. 1984. *Classical Hebrew Poetry: A Guide to its Technique*. Sheffield: JSOT Press.

Wendland, Ernst. 1991. "Oral-Aural Dynamics of the Word." Paper presented at the UBS Triennial Translation Workshop. Victoria Falls, Zimbabwe.

———. 1988 " 'The Word of the Lord' and the Organization of Amos." OPTAT 2:4. pp. 1-51.

Würthwein, Ernst. 1979. *The Text of the Old Testament: An Introduction to the* Biblia Hebraica. Grand Rapids: Eerdmans.

Continuity and Discontinuity in Hebrew Poetic Design: Patterns and Points of Significance in the Structure and Setting of Psalm 30

Ernst R. Wendland

The issue in brief: When "and" is "but"

There is a major turning point that occurs near the middle of Psalm 30 (verse 6a; Hebrew verse 7). It is marked in the original by the emphatic initial pronoun "I" (*'ani*), which is preceded by the common transitional conjunction *waw*. In the present instance, however, as on many other occasions in the Hebrew Bible, this inseparable particle is best translated, not by its normal dictionary gloss, "and," but rather according to its contextual function in the discourse. The composite form that results from the linkage of this conjunction with the foregrounded personal pronoun represents a paradoxical point of progression ("and") coupled with an interruption ("as for me") in the text. The development of the poem is carried forward, but a new and unexpected stage of the poet's argument commences at this juncture (see structural analysis below). In order to highlight this important transition, Craigie renders it as follows: "But I—I (said in my security)" (1983:250). Thus in this context "and" is equivalent to "but." Surprisingly most of the major English versions leave the *waw* untranslated; e.g., GNB: "I felt secure and said . . . ."

The purpose of this study is to explore other prominent instances of such continuity and discontinuity within the text of Psalm 30, following the methodology that was outlined in chapter one. We will observe how these two complementary principles of composition act in tandem, both to organize this particular poetic discourse formally, semantically, as well as pragmatically, and also to characterize many others like it in the literary tradition of ancient Israel. In conclusion some possible theological implications of this important stylistic feature will be briefly considered.

It should be noted at the outset that the pair of compositional strategies examined here are certainly not the only ones which affect literary creation. But they seem to be especially important with regard to poetic discourse in general and Psalm 30 in particular, and so the discussion will be more or less restricted to them. This presentation is further limited by considerations of space. Much more could, and probably should, be said to provide additional background information concerning related studies of continuity and discontinuity along with other stylistic techniques typical of biblical literature. In addition it would have been helpful to be able to explore in somewhat greater detail the implications of their joint operation in artistic works. But the more modest aim of the present chapter is simply to call attention to the complementary interaction of these two outstanding generic aspects of style in Hebrew lyric poetry and to describe their manifestation within the context of a specific poem. A related goal is to evaluate the effect of these devices in terms of communicative significance, particularly when realized in a more natural medium, that is, an oral recital.

Continuity—carrying a text forward and tying it together

The principle of *continuity* is reflected in the tendency of a well-formed composition to manifest the features of progression and coherence. *Progression* has reference to the sense of forward direction that a coherent text exhibits. The discourse is going somewhere, from A to B and even on to Z in a manner that continually advances, unfolds, fulfills, or develops the message. This movement may not be evident immediately, but after several careful readings or hearings it should become apparent to the majority of receptors. Progression may be *syntagmatic* (temporal/consequential) or *paradigmatic* (spatial/descriptive) in nature, and this tendency is normally experienced in some tangible way as one proceeds through the text. Thus one should be able to discern that the author's message is being meaningfully composed and brought to a state of completion, for example, in the form of a narrative, exposition, exhortation, argument, description, or some poetic expression.

The primary ways of organizing a progression in discourse are based on relations of class, time, and space (cp. Nida forthcoming: 6). This includes a number of subcategories that may overlap in their textual realization: *rank* (e.g., greater > lesser, generic > specific), *consequence* (i.e., cause-effect dependencies), and *correlative sequencing* (e.g., positive-negative, question-answer, text-intertext [allusion, quotation]). The more complex the discourse, the more numerous the distinct but interrelated patterns and sequences that are manifested within it on various levels of content and expression. Poetry generally exemplifies a relatively complicated or concentrated sort of arrangement in this regard.

Coherence refers to the characteristics of connectivity, conjunction, and congruence which a text displays with respect to both form and meaning. The result is an impression of unity and harmony in which the whole is clearly greater than, distinct from, or not immediately derivable from the sum of its individual parts. And yet all of the constituent elements fit together appropriately to comprise the composition in its entirety. Coherence may be viewed from both a textual as well as an extratextual perspective. The *textual* aspect may be either formal or semantic in nature, i.e., exhibiting *cohesion* (verbal linkage) and *congruence* (meaningful connection) respectively. In most artistic works both dimensions are present, but one tendency may be emphasized more strongly than its counterpart.

The *extratextual* component of coherence pertains to the real or imagined conceptual world, or cognitive environment, that is both presupposed and evoked by a particular discourse. Of special importance is the perceived relationship (suitability, relevance, applicability, etc.) of the text with the situational milieu and conditions in which it was originally composed and then subsequently transmitted and received. In contrast to the initial event, which is (or was) unique, the context of subsequent performances is obviously flexible and disparate in nature. Thus in cases where the contemporary setting—whether *internal* (cognitive, emotive, volitional) or *external* (historical, sociocultural, geographical, ecological)—differs appreciably from the situation and circumstances that first applied, problems of perception, understanding, appreciation, and evaluation necessarily increase, sometimes to the point where a successful act of communication cannot take place at all.

A crucial factor in the formation of continuity in discourse is *repetition* of one type or another—whether exact or recognizably similar with regard to form, and corresponding or contrastive with regard to meaning (content, intent). This is a compositional strategy which is particularly prominent in poetry, as the following analysis of Psalm 30 will demonstrate. The scope of such replication may be restricted to the individual poetic line (colon) or couplet (bi-/tri-cola); alternatively a much larger structural design may take shape, one which encompasses the entire poem and/or major sections within it.

Furthermore, as a result of the operation of repetition, there is a strong tendency for poetic discourse to be constructed in the form of *patterns*, that is, functionally significant arrangements of elements, on all levels of linguistic organization—sound, sense, and syntax. Phonological patterns are perhaps the most obvious when it comes to poetry, e.g., assonance, alliteration, rhyme, onomatopoeia, paronomasia. Indeed, the demarcation of a text into discrete lines that are related to one another in various ways (i.e., parallelism) and which manifest a perceptible equivalence of sound sequencing by means of a regular rhythmic progression of word-accents (meter), is one of the principal characteristics that distinguishes discourse in the Hebrew Bible as being more poetic or less poetic along a poetic/prosaic continuum.

But the patterned recursion of other features that are formally or semantically related to one another also contributes greatly to the overall effect, such as word endings (e.g., masculine vs. feminine morphemes), lexical stems (including conventionally associated word pairs and merisms), phrases (containing key theological motifs/thematic concepts), and syntactic constructions (especially the order of primary constituents within the colon/clause, i.e., V-S-O, or T-C). Such aesthetically pleasing patterns, which include significant intertextual correspondences and conventional variations such as introversion (chiasmus), usually traverse an entire poem as well as its major and minor constituents. Together, which is how they must always be considered, they function both to *segment* the discourse (the borders of principal units being indicated through the reiteration of significant elements) and also to *synthesize* it, again within a larger framework of recurrent and interrelated form and meaning.

In this way the principle of continuity establishes the essential fabric of a unified poetic composition. It thereby contributes greatly to its overall level of appeal or attractiveness. The overlapping, multilayered sequences and series of patterns serve to constitute the structural foundation or basis upon which other more elaborate discourse features may be fashioned. The latter then form the relief, the figures which stand out from their background to create crucial supplementary special effects, that is, in addition to helping to define the internal boundaries of the whole more completely and precisely.

One particularly important interpersonal effect of continuative techniques in biblical poetry is to support the creation and maintenance of a dynamic interaction between author and audience by means of the verbal imagery and vocal impressions which they hold in common. These operate concurrently within their joint literary tradition and context of communication to stimulate the sensorium in the direction of some significant synthesis with regard to the intended receptor group's fundamental thoughts, values, feelings and/or desires. This cognitive-emotive-volitional environment may pertain temporarily to the past, present, or future; either within or outside of the Temple/Jerusalem area in terms of space; and socially or (in the case of Psalm 30) spiritually with respect to the individual as part of the entire fellowship of God's people, on the one hand, and to the wonderful person, works, and will of Yahweh, on the other.

Discontinuity—breaking up a text and highlighting its contents

The contrastive, foregrounded elements referred to above are introduced through the operation of the opposing yet complementary compositional principle of *discontinuity*. This produces a certain artistic tension into the work, which prevents it from becoming predictable or commonplace with regard to form, content, function, and/or psychological effect. The cohesive, forward-moving progression of similarities needs to be distinguished by being played against periodic differences to achieve a certain balance of literary forces, the ultimate purpose of which is to facilitate a communication (sharing) of the author's intended meaning. Thus, in sum, it is a fine line that the poet must follow: too much continuity and his work becomes banal—predictable and hence boring; too much discontinuity and it fragments and begins to disintegrate, with a consequent decrease or even a complete disruption in the process of cognitive comprehension and aesthetic appreciation on the part of his audience.

The poet has a variety of rhetorical techniques at his disposal in order to inject *points* of discontinuity within the discourse. Their main purpose is to highlight certain prominent aspects of thematic content and to augment the communicative impact which his poem has upon listeners. In general these all involve the interruption of an established pattern and/or the introduction of novelty (surprise) within the text—some overt addition, omission, or shift in expectancy, whether formal or semantic. In Hebrew poetic discourse the principal devices that are employed to introduce discontinuity are *figurative language* (e.g., simile, metaphor, metonymy, hyperbole, personification) and *formal alteration* (e.g., a sudden shift in word order, tense, person, voice, meter, line length, or else literary insertion/lexical redistribution). However, it should be noted here that the effect of these figures of speech is often due to relatively slight variations in what is normally rather conventional religious diction. Similarly the linguistic modifications injected into the text frequently sound more jarring in literal translation than they actually are in the original Hebrew.

Other semantic, syntactic, and/or sonic features that may be employed to defamiliarize the discourse are: the interjection of intensive, imperative, and exclamatory utterances; extended plays on meaning; shifts from/to direct-indirect-embedded speech (quotation and dequotation); rhetorical or deliberative questions; asyndeton and ellipsis; an additional/deleted word or line (colon); irony and paradox; a direct appeal (vocative address) or reference to Yahweh, one's enemies, or to the psalmist himself. It is a regular feature of Hebrew poetic parallelism to find such devices situated in the second [B] line of a bicolon to give it that heightened effect that many scholars have called attention to in recent years.

Poets normally aim at some manner of embellishing a more prosaic discourse as a means of enhancing the impact and appeal of their message. With respect to continuity as earlier described, this will often take the form of a deliberate *expansion* or overlaying of the patterns of verbal repetition employed. With discontinuity, on the other hand, we usually find a marked *concentration* or convergence of stylistic features (special effects) in order to distinguish aspects of extra importance in relation to a poem's structure or theme. Such devices characteristically perform a rhetorical (poetic) purpose by facilitating the carrying out of the principal functions of communication, which in Hebrew texts, as in all literature, are these: expressive, interpersonal (phatic), informative, imperative, performative, and emotive (de Waard and Nida 1986:25-32).

We will now carefully examine the text of Psalm 30 from several analytical perspectives in order to reveal its various patterns of continuity and points of discontinuity. We want to determine how these key poetic principles interact to express what we might posit as being the essential message which the poet, speaking both for himself as well as for the community of faithful worshipers, wished to convey to his God. We will pay special attention to the outstanding oral-aural features of the discourse, on the assumption that this vital audio dimension makes a distinct contribution, not only to the activity of communicating this hymn of praise to Yahweh, but also to the overall meaning-experience that participants derive from its singing, reciting, or chanting—from biblical times even up to the present day (if properly instructed).

This particular psalm was chosen for several reasons: it has not been the object of much scholarly study in the past; it is relatively short; and it appears to consist of a rather simply constructed string of conventional psalmic expressions. But what lies beneath the surface of this seemingly straightforward song of thanksgiving? (On the genre, see Gerstenberg 1988:133.) How do the procedures for analysis outlined in chapter one help us to reveal and evaluate some additional aspects of both its technical artistry as well as its evocative effect? Finally, what are some of the modern techniques of communication which may be pressed into service to help transmit more of the essence of this ancient expression of deeply personal faith and joyous commitment to the "saints" (verse 4) of today?

Contextualizing the text

As in the case of most of the songs in the book of Psalms, it is difficult to pinpoint the original occasion and setting of Psalm 30 with any degree of probability. Nevertheless, in a certain transferred sense we can detect the influence of continuity and discontinuity even here, as one's position on the matter inevitably affects the interpretation that results (Leupold 1959:251). Does the "I" of this psalm represent an individual or a communal voice, or can the former be viewed as merging with the latter as the song develops, from either a synchronic or diachronic perspective? Under what circumstances does he/they utter these words of thankful praise after divine deliverance from some serious crisis or calamity? The initial double designation of genre does not shed much light on the subject, since the two terms appear to be rather closely related, viz. the general *shir*, referring to any type of sung poetic piece, and the more technical *mizmor*, perhaps specifying that the song was to be accompanied by musical instruments (but also based on the verb "sing," *zamar*).

A number of possible contexts have been identified. Considered in isolation they are quite distinct from one another, that is, they are discontinuous with respect to compositional setting. But these situations (and others yet to be discovered) may also be taken together as a group, related by the underlying sequence of generic events which seem to motivate the specific utterances that comprise this psalm (and many other hymns of thanksgiving). The overall pattern runs something like this: *PROBLEM*: person/people sins (e.g., pride) → *CONSEQUENCE* (state of conflict): Yahweh punishes (by means of a hard test/trial, e.g., adversaries/affliction) → *RESPONSE* (to eliminate the conflict): person/people repent and request forgiveness → *CLIMAX*: Yahweh forgives and delivers person/people → *RESOLUTION*: person/people respond with thanksgiving and praise. The details may vary, of course, according to the historical and theological circumstances; for example, concerning the nature of the problem or sin involved (this may be implicit), the type of affliction experienced, the perceived relationship between the psalmist/people and Yahweh as manifested in their response, the nature of his saving act to effect a resolution, and the manner in which the people express their gratitude.

Although the traditional heading to Psalm 30 has been discounted by many scholars, it does provide a possible occasion for the song that has much to commend it. No discourse, whether artistic or not, exists in a vacuum. Its linguistic forms must derive their basic sense and significance from the setting in which they were used. The same text, if situated in another context, can take on a completely different meaning. This is because the scene and situation of its initial composition and/or performance inevitably directs the process of interpretation during reception; e.g., a familiar hymn sung in church (worship) as opposed to a tavern (joke). Rather than viewing these long-standing titles, whether they were original or not, as limiting factors, it is more productive to regard them as an instructive means of "open[ing] up possibilities for interpretation, [since they] suggest a circumstance in which the introduced psalm would be appropriate and thus provide an illustrative clue to interpretation" (Miller 1986:26). Furthermore, "the reading of the Psalms [as] reflected in the superscriptions helps the believing community reapply those texts as pilgrimage songs of faith" (Bellinger 1990:29).

But before one can use the given title as a possible setting for Psalm 30, an apparent situational discontinuity, or ambiguity, first has to be dealt with: which particular "house" did King David "dedicate" [*chanak*] in his day? Though not involved with the actual construction of the first Temple, David did dedicate, or set aside, the site of the future house of God that his son Solomon would later build in his stead (1 Chr 22.1, 6; 2 Chr 3.1). The events leading up to this decision—the king's foolish census of his army, the LORD's plague of judgment upon Israel, David's prayer of repentance, and Yahweh's merciful response—are recorded in 2 Samuel 24 and 1 Chronicles 21. This historical incident could well form the background for David's later poetic reflection on his own sinful pride, which brought disaster upon the nation and might have ended up in is own "descent into the pit," had God actually heeded his intercessory self-imprecation (Psa 30.5-9, 11; cp. 1 Chr 21.13, 17). But the LORD listened to David's appeal on behalf of the people and even spared his own life, thus "removing his sackcloth and clothing him with joy" (Psa 30.11; cp. 1 Chr 21.16, 26).

Other historical reconstructions from the biography of David are possible, but not as likely in the absence of an account of any physical sickness, whether real or threatened, that was associated, for example, with the dedication of his palace in Jerusalem after the establishment of his kingship (2 Sam 5.9-12). It may be of course that the psalm was composed by David in grateful response to some recovery from an unrecorded illness (cp. Psa 6), and that the title was added later in order to contextualize, as it were, the song's use in the cultic setting of Temple worship. There are some striking similarities with King Hezekiah's song of praise after his sickness, recorded in Isaiah 38 (especially verses 14, 17-18, 20). Hezekiah, who was familiar with David's psalms (2 Chr 29.30), seemed to have been especially prone to excessive pride in his life (cp. 2 Chr 32.24-25; Isa 39.2, 8). It may be, therefore, that he attributed his affliction by the LORD to this particular personal weakness (Psa 30.5-7).

It seems likely that Psalm 30, initially composed as an individual prayer of thanksgiving, was subsequently adapted for corporate liturgical use, as suggested in particular by the included exhortation to the "saints" (*chasidim*) to "sing praises to Yahweh" (verses 4-5). This made it appropriate for application to several crucial events in Judah's later history with special reference to their preeminent setting of worship at the "house" of Yahweh. Thus some commentators view the psalm as having been nationalized after the exile in Babylon for ceremonial use at the dedication of the second Temple when it was completed in 515 B.C. (van Gemeren 1991:257). In this case the "healing" (*rafah*) referred to in verse 2 would represent a metaphorical contextualization of the actual situation, viz. Judah's sinfulness (self-righteous pride) → sickness (destruction of Jerusalem and captivity) → national penitence (call to Yahweh for help) → deliverance by Yahweh (defeat of Babylon and the exiles' return to Judea). Three and a half centuries later a similar crisis situation presented itself to renew the relevance of the psalm as a memorial of healing in relation to the Temple, namely, its ritual cleansing and rededication under Judas Maccabaeus from the defilement introduced by Antiochus Epiphanes (Perowne 1878:279). This momentous event is still celebrated by devout Jews today in the Festival of Hanukkah (from *chanak*).

Despite the obvious disparity in the various potential settings surveyed above (and others could no doubt be cited, such as those posited from the perspective of form criticism: e.g., Gerstenberg 1988:135-136), we observe that they are not mutually exclusive. Thus, although it is clear that each situational change would have a significant effect upon specific aspects of the psalm's interpretation (Leupold 1959:251), its basic message remains essentially the same: praise Yahweh for his gracious (*ratson, chanan*) help in the day of trouble. Within the religious poetic literature of Israel, we see this as a good example of the creative extension of a hymn's relevance through its recontextualization with regard to each new setting that seemed appropriate. There are thus elements of both continuity and discontinuity in the historical tradition that forms the essential background against which the psalm must be understood. It has primary reference to the original situation milieu in which it arose, a unique set of events which may no longer be recoverable with certainty, if at all, though the attempt must always be made. One or more subsequent calamities may have provided the impetus for a significant reinterpretation of the text in relation to its contemporary context, and so the process of resetting the scene of the singer's conversation with God can and should be repeated in every new age and cultural milieu.

Thus any psalm "is an historical marker bridging past (initial writing [or composition]) to present (current reading), and embodies a potential future (subsequent reading and interpretation)" (Luke 1988:143). The book of Psalms represents an "unbroken continuity that ties the ancient text to the present" (Miller 1986:22) and the disruptions of life that inevitably occur. Here one can find a reassuring answer or an empathetic human response in the deeply personal, but also profoundly theological, experience which these eminently religious poems evoke. Their scope is universal, i.e., valid and necessary for all people, but their perspective and message is specific, that is, fashioned in the image of the people of Israel's faith-life in and with Yahweh, God of the covenant of unfailing faithfulness (*chesed*).

It is clear that the connotative character of Psalm 30 changes according to the particular setting in which it is applied. For example, as the individual "I" is referentially widened into its representative, communal counterpart, the powerful, intensely personal psychological overtones similarly broaden in scope. These reflect, first of all, a more general anxiety concerning a serious calamity faced by the nation or religious community as a whole, and then joyous optimism for a blessed future due to the timely intervention of a transcendent ("holy," verse 4) but immanent ("favorable," verses 5, 7) God. Likewise the central act of healing may describe a specific bodily affliction, or it can be metaphorically extended to include some other life-threatening danger or crisis. This contextually-determined referential process may be extended further to encompass any profoundly depressing psychological or spiritual experience. Hence the contemporary relevance of the book of Psalms to believers of every age.

The tension inherent in this specific-generic (individual-communal) dichotomy with regard to the setting of use (composition, translation, [reception]) is an important aspect of the full communicative significance of each individual psalm. Thus the ambiguity over the set of circumstances surrounding the creation of Psalm 30 forces analysts today to consider seriously the implications of contextual continuity and discontinuity and its effect upon the message being communicated, then and now. Subjectivity (and uncertainty) is inevitably involved, but so is a certain degree of freedom to put oneself into the place of the psalmist in order to better understand and empathize with his deeply-felt physical and spiritual situation—the personal crisis and its final resolution due to gracious provision of Yahweh. As a guide in this exercise of contextualization, it helps to make the effort to familiarize oneself not only with the song's diverse historical, sociocultural, and theological background as hypothetically outlined above, but also with its prominent literary and linguistic characteristics. It is to this latter, textual setting that we now turn in order to derive more concrete insights into the rhetorical dynamics of this timeless lyric tribute to the LORD's holy favor in a time of testing.

Textualizing the discourse by means of its cotext

Before one can analyze a biblical passage, it is usually necessary to make an effort to determine exactly what constitutes the original text. This is a particular problem in the case of the Hebrew Scriptures, because the only reliable external manuscript evidence available for comparative purposes is that offered by the Dead Sea Scrolls, supplemented by the textual tradition which is reflected, albeit indirectly, in the Septuagint (LXX) translation. A book such as the Psalms presents further complications, since it is a composite production, covering a long historical period and a multiple, ever-changing literary as well as religious tradition. But it is important for interpreters to make an attempt at least to establish what the original might have been in cases of diversity, ambiguity, or obscurity, in order to keep the subjectivity of their analysis to a minimum.

A simple textual principle which helps the most to achieve objectivity is one that presupposes the general reliability of the Masoretic Text (MT). Accordingly it is assumed to be correct as received unless conclusively proven to be in error, on the one hand, and amenable to a genuinely valid alternative reading on the other. In particular proposed emendations based upon the supposed meter of the Hebrew are discounted, for all such argumentation is patently circular and hence overly tolerant of idiosyncrasy. An example of this sort of reckless approach to the text is Oesterley's several proposed omissions from Psalm 30 on the grounds that they "overload the half-line" (1959:203).

Space does not allow us to take up a complete form- or text-critical study of Psalm 30 here. In any case the problems are relatively few and not all that crucial to one's understanding of the poem. We might just point out a few of the major areas of controversy to illustrate the necessity of considering both the context and the cotext of the passage in question in order to determine the most probable reading and possibly also to explain how certain alternatives might have arisen. In terms of our overall analytical perspective, such *variants* represent points of *discontinuity* which interrupt the smooth transmission of the poet's intended message, and therefore they need to be addressed at least, if not conclusively resolved.

The first significant difficulty concerns the second-last word of verse 3 (Hebrew, verse 4). The *kethiv* is *miyyoredey*, literally "from the ones going down" (i.e., into the pit), whereas the *qere* suggests a somewhat irregular infinitive construct plus suffix: *miyyordi* "from my going down." Modern English versions seem to be divided on the issue, viz. "I was on my way to the depths below" (GNB), "(spared) me from going down" (NIV), versus "from among those who sink (into oblivion)" (New Jerusalem Bible [NJB]), "from among those gone down" (New Revised Standard Version [NRSV]). The majority of commentators, along with the LXX, support the *kethiv*.

In this instance there are three additional pieces of evidence that would tend to lend preference to the text as written. They are given in the usual order of importance when evaluating such matters:

a) *Internal cotext*: the normal form of the infinitive construct of *yarad* occurs in verse 9—a passage which parallels verse 3 in the pattern of introversion that structures this text as a whole (see below), i.e., *beridti* "in my going down." Thus an alternative form, as indicated here by the *qere*, is not likely within the same discourse (cp. Craigie 1983:251).

b) *External cotext*: the expression "from those going down into the pit" is formulaic in nature and is found elsewhere in an analogous form in the book of Psalms. We note especially a similar passage in Psalm 28, namely, verse 1: "with those going down [into the pit]" (which in turn is exactly the same as Psa 143.7).

c) *Situational context*: If the hypothetical setting proposed above in accordance with the psalm's assigned title is valid, then a plural reference is more likely here than the personal singular. Thus "those who went down into the grave" would be a poetic description of the 70,000 men who died as a result of the plague which David's proud census provoked upon Israel (1 Chr 21.14). The LORD mercifully spared the perpetrator himself, the royal poet, who gratefully responds with this song of self-censure and divine praise (1 Chr 21.13; cp. Psa 30.2-3).

In this case it is not difficult to understand how an initial reference to others—whether the king's subjects, the casualties of the calamity, or the dead in general—could get reinterpreted more narrowly to denote either the poet himself (e.g., at a time of grave illness) or the nation as a whole (i.e., the communal "I" in crisis).

Commentators struggle with the complex, multiple contrastive parallelism of verse 5, especially in the initial bicolon, which appears to involve some syntactic problems, viz. "for in his anger [is] a moment; in his favor [is] a life[time]." The term usually chosen for alteration is the first noun *rega'* "moment." Some (e.g., Dahood, followed by Craigie 1983:251 and van Gemeren 1991:260) reinterpret the word to mean "death," perhaps because it often occurs in the cotext of God's judgment and the grave in the Old Testament, as in the immediately preceding verses (Psa 30.1-3). A similar proposal to emphasize the antithesis of the parallelism involves emendation, that is, to the noun *nega'* "plague/ stroke" (Gunkel and apparatus, followed by Oesterley 1959:302), i.e., "for in his anger [is] a plague." Such a rendering would of course nicely fit the contextual setting proposed above to fit the psalm's title, namely, the calamity which befell Jerusalem (1 Chr 21.15).

In favor of the traditional interpretation, however, which is retained more or less by most modern versions, is first of all the temporal focus of the immediate (internal) cotext, i.e., "in the night" and "to/at the morning" of verse 6b. The wider (external) cotext also would support such an understanding; for example, those texts that refer to the passing of time in relation to one's afflictions (e.g., Psa 31.15; 32.3-4). There are in particular several passages in Isaiah that refer specifically to the LORD's transient anger in contrast to his everlasting mercy; e.g., 26.20; 54.7-8.

Thus, in balance, since there is no really conclusive evidence to the contrary, it is better to remain with the MT's reading.

A pair of disputed terms are juxtaposed in the second half of the long initial colon of verse 7. The form of the main verb in MT (a hiphil perfect) is anomalous: *he'emadtah* "you caused . . . to (take a) stand," namely, the final consonant. Therefore most proposed emendations (e.g., Oesterley 1959:203) suggest replacing it with the first person singular object suffix, i.e., "you made me stand" (e.g., NRSV). But the text as it reads could be interpreted simply as being an emphatic poetic form complementing the foregrounded object *'oz* "strength."

This boastful assertion is then completed by the locative *leharri* (lit.) "to/for my mountain," a form that some emend to "my beauty" (e.g., LXX) and others revocalize to the plural construct, "the mountains of" (e.g., Craigie 1983:251). Again, MT may be meaningfully construed as written, without change, literally "O LORD, you caused strength to take a stand for my mountain." This would be a picturesque way of reiterating what was just said in the preceding colon, i.e., "I will never be moved!" (cp. *Preliminary and Interim Report on the Hebrew Old Testament Text Project* [HOTTP] 3:209). A similar expression occurs in a corresponding cotext in Psa 18.33 (lit.) "and upon my high places he (Yahweh) causes me to take my stand/to stand firm." If the original contextual situation proposed above is correct, the reference here could well be to the hill country of Jerusalem, or even to its royal citadel, where King David probably was residing when he made his fateful proclamation of a military census (cp. 1 Chr 21.4-5, 15; Psa 125.1-2).

A final example to illustrate the influence of context and cotext upon the interpretation of a given text occurs in verse 9 with the expression *bedami* "in my blood." Some prefer to repoint the consonants to read *bedomi* "in my weeping" (e.g., Craigie 1983:251; van Gemeren 1991:262), apparently to establish a parallel with verses 5b and 12a. There are a number of literary and linguistic reasons, however, which would argue against such a proposal. First of all, the most proximate parallel of this word is found in the immediately following words of the next colon: "in my going down into the pit." The latter is obviously a figurative description of death, as is "in my blood." A similar double reference to the grave appeared earlier in verse 3, a passage that parallels 9 in the structural introversion that encompasses this psalm.

Secondly, the meaning (II) "weep, wail" for the verb *damam* is poorly attested, and it could be argued that there is only a single main sense, viz. "be[come] silent, still" (Brown-Driver-Briggs). This meaning fits just as well in verse 12, while in verse 6 a different verb altogether is used, i.e., *bakah* "weep, wail." Any extratextual setting that is postulated for Psalm 30 could support either reading, although the graphic "my blood" would seem to be more likely. Indeed, from a divine perspective, as rhetorically adopted by the poet, some salutary purpose would most certainly derive from a person's shedding tears of repentance (verses 5, 11), but surely not from his complete demise (verse 9)—or silence (verse 12)!

As the preceding examples would suggest, the most appropriate or probable solution in the case of textual problems is not normally the easiest. Thus it is not necessarily the one that results in a more "continuous" text—one which serves to smooth over or eliminate apparent "discontinuities" in MT that cannot be easily explained or accommodated to either the cotext or an assumed situational context. Rather it is the reading that is substantiated by a variety of criteria, formal as well as functional, beginning from evidence found in the immediate verbal environment and extending from there to any clues that may be apparent among the significant structural points and patterns manifested by the composition as a whole. After a brief consideration of the nature of poetic construction in general, we will turn to a closer examination of the larger discourse framework of Psalm 30.

What is "poetry"?

> *The poetic function [of language] projects the principle of equivalence from the axis of selection into the axis of combination.* (Jakobson 1960:358)

For over three decades now (cp. Zevit 1990) this well-known poetic dictum has engaged a host of literary scholars in the attempt both to interpret and apply it in the analysis of specific works and also to evaluate its suitability and relevance as a characterization of poetry. One of the most useful of such studies is Adele Berlin's investigation of the nature and operation of biblical parallelism (1985:7-17). The purpose here is not to make a review of the extensive literature on the subject (for that, see the two references cited above), but rather to suggest a minor elaboration of the principle. Accordingly we will attempt to redefine it in terms of the analytical notions introduced in this essay, and more significantly, then, to adopt such a perspective in our effort to explore certain prominent aspects of the textual organization and communicative dynamics of Psalm 30.

The term "equivalence" has often been misunderstood as referring only to linguistic similarities (e.g., Berlin 1985:11), and Jakobson himself seemed to emphasize this feature in his various analyses. However, in its original context (Jakobson 1960:358) it is clear that he meant it to include the opposing idea of dissimilarity. Hence equivalence as an expression of what is equal in quantity, quality, form, or function incorporates both correspondence and contrast. *Correspondences*, in turn, establish patterns of continuity in discourse, while *contrasts* fix points of discontinuity. And each of these literary and linguistic strategies operates on both a vertical plane (the paradigmatic "axis of selection") as well as a horizontal plane (the syntagmatic "axis of combination") to constitute the complete text. "Poetry" is therefore distinct from "prose" (i.e., more or less, depending on the nature of the language and genre) in that the principle of equivalence is superimposed upon, or conjoined with, that of combination to such a degree that it becomes equal if not greater as a significant structuring force within the discourse. It is thus a matter of concentration: the various equivalences of sound, sense, and syntax are considerably more numerous than one finds in prose. This characteristic not only draws attention to the special formal nature of poetic discourse, but it also contributes to the higher degree of unity and organization that is typical of poetry as well as its greater semantic density and emotive depth.

The crucial linguistic features which, by their *recursion* in a text, serve to establish such poetic equivalence (whether analogous or antithetical in nature) may involve all four basic types of discourse organization. These may be ranked according to their usual order of perceptibility (and perhaps also translatability) as follows: lexical-semantic (e.g., the use of synoyms and antonyms); syntactic (e.g., the principal sequence of clausal constituents); morphological (e.g., a progression of tense/number/gender, etc.); and finally, phonological (e.g., alliteration, punning). The recognition factor is important because there is a serious question concerning the real function of certain intricate patterns that some structuralist scholars posit but which the vast majority of receptors do not even realize are present in a given poetic composition. This pertains especially to those involving sound, unless they happen to be associated somehow with the sense of related items in the discourse (Zevit 1990:389-90).

The abstract axiom—equivalence superimposed upon sequence of form and meaning—is reflected more concretely in the notion of *parallelism,* which in one verbal manner and means or another characterizes more from less "poetic" works in every language. In Hebrew poetry, for example, this is normally manifested in the series of coupled lines, or cola, which comprise a given text. A particular couplet, whether consisting of the usual two or sometimes more lines, may be *contiguous* or *detached* in nature, as illustrated in the (hypothetical and greatly simplified) schematic diagram below. In this figure, **W,X,Y,** and **Z** symbolize individual words (accent-units) that manifest one or more reiterated and equivalent linguistic features (i.e., phonological, morphemic-affixal, syntactic, or lexical-semantic); a [O] refers to a word having no significant feature that either corresponds or contrasts with those mentioned above; and a [//] indicates a colon-demiline boundary:

WXYZ//**ZWX**//**XY**O//OOO//OO//OOO//OOO//
O**YZW**//**X**O**Z**//OO//OOO//OO//OOO//OOO//
OOZ//**WX**//

This formulaic sequence would suggest a poem of 16 lines. It leads off with a 4:3:3 tricolon and ends with a 3:2 bicolon that features three elements, Z-W-X, which are parallel to those occurring initially in the text (i.e., an *inclusio*). The discourse appears to be divided up into two equal parts (stanzas) of eight lines each, with the final monocolon of part one (OYZW) also exhibiting an *inclusio* through resonance with its beginning. In addition, the first line of stanza two (XOZ) illustrates another important point of equivalence in the form of detached parallelism with the initial line of the poem (i.e., similar unit openings = *anaphora*) and also the feature of a hinge or overlap construction (*anadiplosis*) with the immediately preceding line (i.e., in the repeated Z element). Finally, the endings of both stanzas have similarities, too (i.e., OYZW and OZWX), a structural correspondence termed *epiphora.*

In the case of most poetry, the factor of equivalence also governs the mode of syntagmatic combination with respect to the feature of balanced lineation. There is a phonological (rhythmic) constraint that operates in a more or less rigorous fashion to determine the syntactic limits of line length. Biblical verse is somewhat fluid in this regard, the average colon ranging between two and five word-accent units (average is 3). The regularity manifested in the Hebrew poetic tradition is not tightly symmetrical nor as rigidly controlled as in other literatures. But it is a significant feature nevertheless, for it helps to account for another prominent characteristic of such discourse, namely, its *conciseness* or terseness. The result in terms of style is a formally and semantically condensed mode of expression in which each word, indeed every single morpheme, is carefully positioned to play an essential part in generating the concentrated message that the poet wishes to convey, whether directly or implicitly by allusion.

A genuine poem thus embodies a dense but dynamic communications *network* in which associative (connotative, expressive, aesthetic) meaning plays a crucial role. It is a complete, unified verbal composition consisting of many interwoven and overlapping syntagmatic (horizontal) and paradigmatic (vertical) arrangements, which correspondingly manifest an amplified yet integrated system of semantic operations and pragmatic functions. Individual instances of continuity and discontinuity permeate the whole, variously combining and interacting with each other to structure the discourse more intricately by means of prominent patterns and points of significance. Such an artistically embellished form serves in turn to magnify the work's overall communicative potential—cognitively, emotively, and volitionally as well. Both compositional forces are necessary, for patterns cannot be formed without points (to establish limits and boundaries), while points have no meaning in isolation from larger patterns of linguistic organization. We turn now for illustration to an examination to some of the major global strategies of arrangement and formatting that are exhibited in Psalm 30.

Continuity and discontinuity in the discourse organization of Psalm 30

> *There is little agreement on the structure of the psalm. The parts follow closely on one another without clearly defined literary markers.* (van Gemeren 1991:257-58)

The author of the preceding rather pessimistic assessment of the structure of Psalm 30 is certainly correct in calling attention to the general disagreement manifested by various versions and commentaries with respect to this text. But his further implication that the organization of this psalm is ill-defined can be shown to be in error by a careful analysis of how skillfully the discourse has in fact been composed. Problems arise in this regard because not one structure is involved but several—each neatly superimposed upon the other to enhance the artistry of poetic form and also to increase both the semantic depth and the emotive impact of the work as an instance of profound theological communication. Thus simultaneously operating patterns of continuity and points of discontinuity are expertly blended and balanced in order to effect the poet's larger purpose, which is to sing a song of grateful thanksgiving and praise to Yahweh, who has mercifully delivered him from the threat of death. A number of discourse perspectives are therefore necessary to reveal the basic elements of this complex, rhetorically motivated poetic organization.

I. Linear-surface structure

We will begin by presenting the structural arrangement which is perhaps the most obvious, namely, that of the temporal progression of poetic lines, or cola (figure I). This textual analysis is based upon a prior translation and spatialization of the entire psalm (cp. steps 3-4, chapter 1 of this monograph). The English represents a relatively literal word-for-word rendering of the original. The individual words joined by hyphens indicate what constitutes a single lexical/rhythmic unit in Hebrew. The numbers in parentheses then give the number of such units, or "words," in each line of a given bi-/tricolon, and these lines are referred to by the letters "a," "b," and "c" after the respective verse numbers along the right-hand margin.

(Figure I)

[A]	I-will-exalt-you, Yahweh, for you-lifted-me-out,		1.a
	and-not=did-you-let-rejoice my-enemies over-me.	(4+3)	.b
	Yahweh, my-God, I-cried-for-help to-you and-you-healed-me.		2.a
	Yahweh, you-brought-up from-sheol my-soul.		3.b
	You-kept-me-alive from-those-descending-into the pit.	(5+4+3)	.c
[B]	Sing-praise to-Yahweh, his-pious-ones,		4.a
	and-give-thanks for-the-memory-of his-holiness.	(3+3)	.b
	For a-moment [is] in-his-anger,		5.a
	life [is] in-his-favor.	(3+2)	.b
	In-the-evening it-endures weeping,		.a
	and-at-the-morning [is] a-joyous-shout.	(3+2)	.b
[C]	And-I I-said in-my-security,		6.a
	"Not-shall-I-be-moved forever!	(3+2)	.b
	Yahweh, in-your-favor you-caused-[it]-to-take-a-stand for-my-mountain [namely] strength!"		7.a
	You-hid your-face, I-was dismayed!	(5+4)	.b
[D]	Unto-you, Yahweh, I-will-call,		8.a
	and-unto-my-Lord I-will-plead-for-mercy.	(3+2)	.b
	What-profit [is] in-my-blood,		9.a
	in-my-descending into-destruction?	(2+2)	.b
	Will-it-thank-you the-dust,		.a
	will-it-proclaim your-faithfulness?	(2+2)	.b
	Hear-O-Yahweh and-show-mercy-to-me!		10.a
	O-Yahweh, be a-helper for-me!	(3+3)	.b
[E]	You-turned my-wailing into-dancing for-me.		11.a
	you-removed my-sackcloth, and-you-clothed-me-with joy	(4+4)	.b
	so-that it-may-sing-praise-to-you [my]-glory and-not it-will-be-silent.		12.a
	Yahweh, my-God, forever I-will-thank-you!	(5+4)	.b

Four major breaks in the discourse are indicated, that is, after verses 3, 5, 7, and 10. These represent points of noteworthy disjunction, or discontinuity, in the text, which is then divided into five segments or "strophes," i.e., [A] 1-3, [B] 4-5, [C] 6-7, [D] 8-10, and [E] 11-12. There are clear formal and semantic markers that serve to delineate the beginning (aperture [*ap.*]) and/or ending (closure [*cl.*]) of each unit. These may be summarized as follows (only several of the main cohesive devices are mentioned):

[A]—*ap.* the psalm begins; emphatic introduction, an initial summons to praise, indicates psalm type, i.e., a eulogy

cl. the ending of a series of relatively long cola giving the motivation for praise, featuring references to the grave; to the singer, i.e., first person pronominal forms (with assonance); to the addressee, i.e., Yahweh (3 vocatives), and to their joint adversaries

[B]—*ap.* imperative opener; shift in addressees ("saints"); Yahweh referred to in the third person; *anaphora* (similar beginning) with verse 1a

cl. conclusion of pair of contrasting bicola; condensed, climactic ending ("a-joyous-shout!"); close of /b+/r/ alliterative sequence

[C]—*ap.* emphatic initial independent pronoun preceded by *waw* ("and-I"); shift in topical focus to self (speaker)

cl. sudden change in tone/mood (i.e., from optimistic to pessimistic), accented by the final, autoreferential word "dismayed!" preceded by asyndeton

[D]—*ap.* front-shifted pronoun with vocative ("unto-you O-Yahweh"); change in tense-aspect (to imperfect); the cola shorten in average length

cl. closing content mirrors that of the beginning (i.e., A-B-A' ring structure), including a double reference to Yahweh

[E]—*ap.* shift in tense-aspect (to perfect) which reflects the sudden transition in mood from sorrow to joy, and in illocution from appeal (verse 10) to praise (verse 11); the metrical pattern lengthens again

cl. final emphatic colon, i.e., asyndeton + vocative with a double mention of the divine name + shift in word order, echoes the initial one of the psalm (*inclusio*); the song ends

There are a number of modern English translations that match the particular discourse segmentation proposed above, e.g., GNB, NIV, NRSV. But it is also important to draw attention to the essential *unity* of the psalm as a whole (an aspect of poetry which most versions and many commentaries fail to do justice to). There are thus a number of patterns of continuity that serve to interrelate the five constituent stanzas and also to bind them into a song that manifests a harmony of structure, theme, and purpose. These features are revealed by the following analytical charts, which offer several different but complementary perspectives on this highly expressive theological composition.

II. Relational-syntagmatic structure

Figure II presents a display of the sequence of basic propositions which comprise Psalm 30 according to its principal discourse divisions (strophes). They are designated by verse numbers (English text) with decimals along the right side of the diagram. Observe first of all that these individual event-/state-centered units are distinct from the poetic lines, or cola, which demarcate the discourse according to rhythmic and/ or syntactic criteria (cp. figure I). A second important feature of the following diagram is that, like the preceding, it presents a literal wording of the Hebrew surface structure. The propositions are not restated in a simplified semantic form as is the usual practice in such analyses (cp. Beekman et. al. 1981:65), e.g., "for-mercy" [8.3] = that you might have mercy on me; "the dust" [9.5] = if I die (demetaphorization). This has been done in order to facilitate a comparison between this and the other charts. It should also be noted that in some instances a more precise semantic breakdown could have been made, especially in the case of delimitive or qualificational propositions (ibid:112), e.g., "his holiness" [4.4] = he is holy. The detail was spared, however, in order to render the display more manageable and perceptible.

(Figure II)

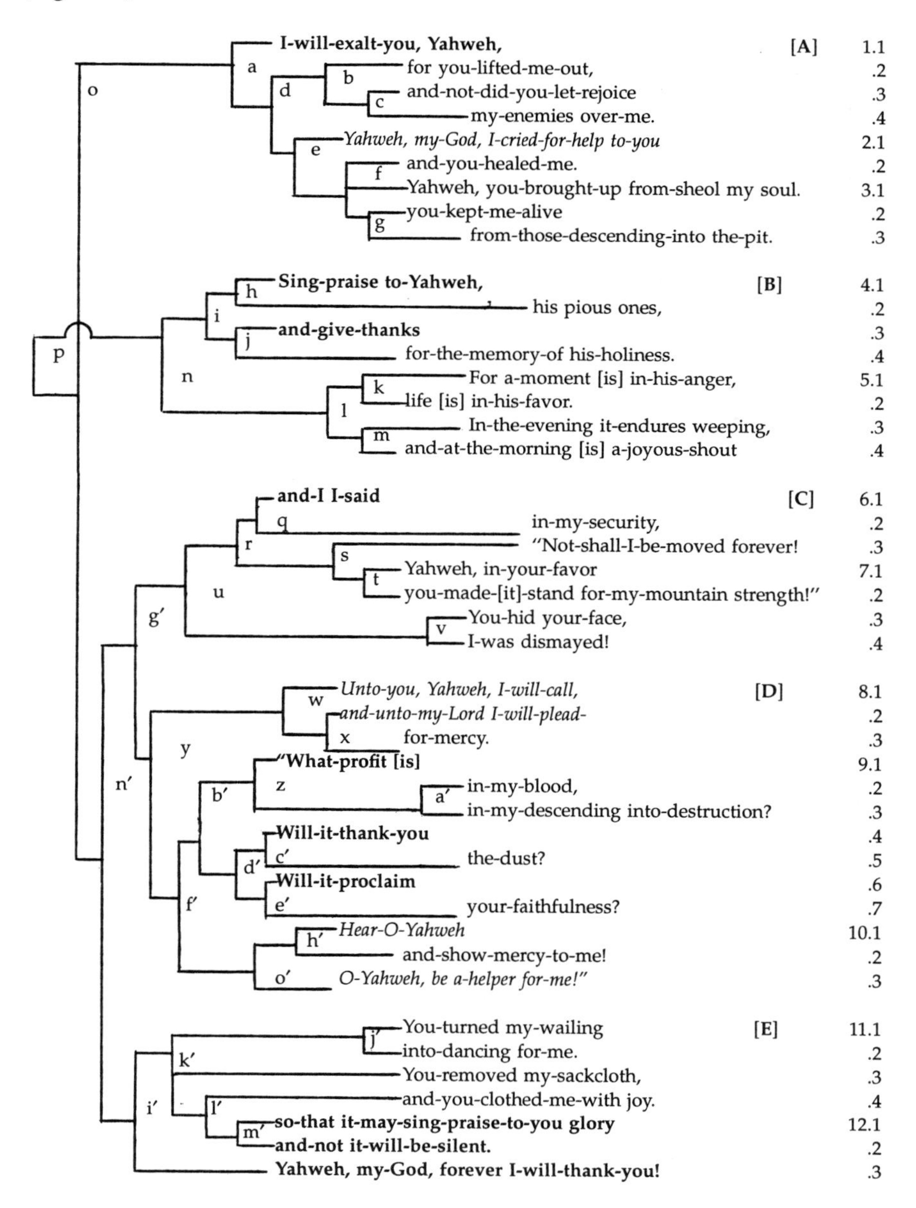
I-will-exalt-you, Yahweh,
[A]
1.1
for you-lifted-me-out,
.2
and-not-did-you-let-rejoice
.3
my-enemies over-me.
.4
Yahweh, my-God, I-cried-for-help to-you
2.1
and-you-healed-me.
.2
Yahweh, you-brought-up from-sheol my soul.
3.1
you-kept-me-alive
.2
from-those-descending-into the-pit.
.3
Sing-praise to-Yahweh,
[B]
4.1
his pious ones,
.2
and-give-thanks
.3
for-the-memory-of his-holiness.
.4
For a-moment [is] in-his-anger,
5.1
life [is] in-his-favor.
.2
In-the-evening it-endures weeping,
.3
and-at-the-morning [is] a-joyous-shout
.4
and-I I-said
[C]
6.1
in-my-security,
.2
"Not-shall-I-be-moved forever!
.3
Yahweh, in-your-favor
7.1
you-made-[it]-stand for-my-mountain strength!"
.2
You-hid your-face,
.3
I-was dismayed!
.4
Unto-you, Yahweh, I-will-call,
[D]
8.1
and-unto-my-Lord I-will-plead-
.2
for-mercy.
.3
"What-profit [is]
9.1
in-my-blood,
.2
in-my-descending into-destruction?
.3
Will-it-thank-you
.4
the-dust?
.5
Will-it-proclaim
.6
your-faithfulness?
.7
Hear-O-Yahweh
10.1
and-show-mercy-to-me!
.2
O-Yahweh, be a-helper for-me!"
.3
You-turned my-wailing
[E]
11.1
into-dancing for-me.
.2
You-removed my-sackcloth,
.3
and-you-clothed-me-with joy.
.4
so-that it-may-sing-praise-to-you glory
12.1
and-not it-will-be-silent.
.2
Yahweh, my-God, forever I-will-thank-you!
.3
a
b
c
d
e
f
g
h
i
j
k
l
m
n
o
p
q
r
s
t
u
v
w
x
y
z
a′
b′
c′
d′
e′
f′
g′
h′
i′
j′
k′
l′
m′
n′
o′

a. implication-grounds
b. base-addition
c. orienter-content
d. base-amplification
e. means-result
f. base-restatement
g. means-result
h. concept-description
i. base-addition
j. implication-grounds
k. base-contrast
l. base-addition
m. base-contrast
n. implication-grounds
o. base-amplification
p. grounds-implication
q. base-circumstance
r. orienter-content
s. base-restatement
t. means-result
u. concession-contraexpectation
v. reason-result
w. base-equivalent
x. orienter-content
y. orienter-content
z. consequence-condition
a′ base-equivalent
b′ base-restatement
c′ consequence-condition
d′ base-restatement
e′ orienter-content
f′ grounds-implication
g′ reason-result
h′ base-addition
i′ grounds-implication
j′ base-contrast
k′ base-restatement
l′ means-purpose
m′ base-contrast
n′ base-progression
o′ base-restatement

The hierarchical, syntagmatic network of interpropositional connections is shown by the solid lines along the left margin of the preceding diagram. The associated series of individual letters refers to the various semantic relationships that link propositional couplets and clusters on the different levels of the structural hierarchy. These relationships are listed in ordered pairs according to their respective designative letters after the propositional display (adapted from Beekman et al. 1981: chapter 8). The different degrees of indentation mark what appear to be five principal levels of thematic dependency within the discourse (cp. section III below).

The results of a relational-syntagmatic (or semantic-structural) analysis of Psalm 30 clearly indicate that the traditional system of designating the meaningful relations between cola (e.g., "synonymous," "contrastive," "synthetic," etc.) is totally inadequate. It can tell us virtually nothing about how the poet has constructed his message, either on the micro- or the macrolevel of the discourse. In order to gain such information, a much finer and more systematically organized semantic grid is necessary, such as that illustrated above (other analytical inventories and schema are of course possible).

A careful examination of the preceding syntagmatic structure reveals that there are five major clusters of propositions which are conjoined to form the complete composition, i.e., verses 1-3 (a-g), verses 4-5 (h-m), verses 6-7 (q-v), verses 8-10 (w-h′), and verses 11-12 (i′-n′). These correspond with the stanza divisions posited earlier for the linear-surface structure on the basis of the formal and semantic markers that highlight points of closure and aperture in the text (figure I). Of special significance here are the larger-level relations which serve to link the five stanzas (A–E) to one another and also to the discourse in its entirety. These logical connections represent essential patterns of meaning continuity that override, as it were, the internal areas of disjunction and establish the psalm as an integral, aesthetic whole—a unified artistic and theological hosanna from the LORD's *chasidim*.

Beginning with the most closely connected stanzas, [C] (verses 6-7) is linked to [D] (verses 8-10) by the semantic relationship of *reason-result* (g′). In other words, the poet's pride (or overconfidence) and subsequent sudden downfall [C] motivated him (i.e., *cause-effect*) to call upon Yahweh, a plea which is recorded in [D]. The outcome of [C] and [D] is then lauded in [E], a *base-progression* relationship (n′). This series of three stanzas would be a good example of what Robert Alter terms the "narrative movement" that characterizes the larger development of many psalms—"a dynamic process moving toward some culmination" (1987: 620). In the case of Psalm 30, this movement begins with a steady state followed by a crisis [C], intensification that leads to an emotive climax [D], then a divinely initiated turning point or reversal and a final resolution [E].

The key to understanding the overall organization of this psalm lies in a recognition of the next relationship, namely, the one that links the first [A] to the final three stanzas [C-E]. In essence the former [A] acts as the basis for the latter triad, i.e., *base-amplification* (o). After an initial repetitive statement of the song's content and intent, the psalmist goes on to artistically elaborate upon this theme in the second half of his song of praise [C-E]—a poetic instance of semantic recycling, or we might say, parallelism on the discourse level!

Only stanza [B] remains, forming the psalm's major point of disjunction as the poet unexpectedly (at first impression) breaks off to urge his fellow saints to join in the song of thanksgiving. After the initial stanza he steps out of his poetic text, as it were, to address the context in a persuasive appeal to those who were apparently present with him on the scene of worship. And yet, set within the discourse as a whole, the discontinuity is smoothed over—or better, is skillfully blended into the compositional structure in its entirety. Stanza [B] thus forms a fitting response, i.e., *grounds-implication* (p), to *both* stanza [A] and also to its recapitulation and expansion in stanzas [C-E]. It is a general, communal exhortation that is based on the poet's individual relationship and personal experience with Yahweh, his covenant LORD.

As written, then [B] acts as the structural pivot that bridges the song's two unequal portions, but it may have been the psalmist's intention that this stanza would actually be repeated after [E] to conclude the larger second half as well. In any case, even if it is not reiterated as a refrain at the end, stanza [B] is certainly not misplaced or superfluous if considered in relation to the cotext in its surrounding totality. This will become more evident as we consider the results of a more synchronically oriented analysis of Psalm 30.

III. Topical-paradigmatic structure

We may begin an investigation of the synchronic patterns that further organize Psalm 30 by referring once more to the five horizontal levels of indentation indicated on the preceding diachronic display (II). These variations serve to distribute the song's sequence of propositions according to the following spatial arrangement:

Level 1—utterances invoking **praise**/thanksgiving to Yahweh
    Level 2—**prayer**/appeal to Yahweh's for help
        Level 3—**proclamation** of Yahweh's deliverance
            Level 4-lament over the LORD's acts of **punishment**
                Level 5—personal expressions of **pride**

Several significant observations can now be made. The psalm begins and ends with a forceful utterance that manifests its dominant illocutionary force and establishes its basic generic nature and overall emotive tone as a *panegyric* poem: thanksgiving and praise (1.1/12.3, i.e., a text-funtional *inclusio*).

This joyful note of celebration is reiterated at two other points in the discourse. These appear in significantly different modes of formal expression, but in places that similarly balance one other within the structure as a whole: 4.1-4 (hortatory plural imperatives) and 9.1-7 (a series of three rhetorical questions that highlight the positive event by suggesting the possibility of its negative counterpart). The latter segment [plea] contrasts in communicative intent with the former [praise], and together with its continuation in verse 10, it may have formed part of a conventional prayer that the psalmist uttered as part of the temple ritual undertaken during his time of trial (cp. Psa 6.5; 28.1; 88.10-12; 115.17; 142.1; Craigie 1983:254). It should also be noted that 12.3 is actually the climax of a triad of functionally equivalent expressions, this independent assertion being preceded by an antithetically stated dependent bicolon of purpose (12.1-2). The major propositions comprising this preeminent paradigmatic strand, which is marked by a repetition of the thematic verb *yadah* ("praise"), are set off in bold type in figure II.

Turning then to level 2 in the synchronic alignment, we observe that these are propositions in which, first of all, the psalmist directs various petitions to Yahweh for help in his hour of need. In relation to level 1, they represent several steps back in time, referring to the dark, troubled period in his life, when all seemed lost, when he was seemingly about ready to "descend into sheol." This motif is only briefly articulated in the first half of the psalm (2.1), but it reaches a much fuller level of expression in the second half, i.e., 8.1-3 and 10.1-3 (the pertinent material is indicated by italics in figure II). Notice that the final pair of propositions (10.2-3) reiterates semantic elements from the preceding two (2.1/8.3), excluding the repeated vocative of address to the LORD. Within the framework of this interpretation, it is proposed that verses 9 and 10 be construed as an actual verbalization of the poet's appeal. It is helpful, therefore, to distinguish these words of direct speech, at least typographically, by means of quotation marks (cp. GNB, NIV). We have here in these two verses an instance of thematic overlapping, as levels 1 (praise) and 2 (prayer) merge with one another.

Synchronic structures 3 (proclamation) and 4 (punishment) may be considered together, since they are antithetical in nature and are regularly conjoined in the discourse of Psalm 30 (as well as in other thanksgiving psalms). Thus the singer offers these assertions as the grounds, or basis, for his words of praise (level 1). The LORD in his mercy delivered the psalmist from sickness and death, thereby also preserving him from the mockery of their common enemies (i.e., the impious or unrighteous). The grateful poet's testimony of faith is proclaimed most strongly in the first and last stanzas (A/E), while the matter of Yahweh's prior chastisement is broached only indirectly by way of contrast, especially through several descriptive references to mourning and the grave. This antithesis is foregrounded also in the two internal stanzas (B/D). Yahweh has graciously preserved the poet from what might have been—from an angry judgment and consequent weeping (verse 5), from blood, destruction, and dust (verse 9). The psalm's central life–death polarity is figuratively reinforced by its pervasive positively-inclined, uplifting imagery: from down to up, sickness to health, night to day, and sorrow to joy (Craghan 1985:178).

We thus arrive at stanza C (6.1–7.4) and the structural center of Psalm 30, where we encounter a point of sudden reversal, a dramatic shift with respect to both form and content. Indeed, there is also a certain measure of irony here as the psalmist initiates a word of praise to himself (hence the indentation to level 1) and even cites Yahweh in support of his secure position (7.1-2, at synchronic level 3). He confidently views his future as being "immoveable" on account of the apparently inalienable "favor" of Yahweh (a blatant expression of pride, level 5). This particular segment of the discourse exhibits another interesting feature, one that is in fact crucial to the understanding of the psalm's larger form and content. Here we have an instance of structural irony, as it were, since this compositional core of the text, a place which normally reveals its thematic peak, in this case represents its spiritual pit and emotional nadir (cp. figure III below). We hear the poet condemn himself with his own words as he boasts of his safe and sure situation in relation to any potential adversary or adversity. This attitude and manifestation of self-sufficiency in the very presence of Yahweh served to precipitate the major catastrophe in his life.

According to this interpretation, then, the segment of direct (embedded) discourse begun at 6.3 does not end there (as all English versions indicate) but rather continues through 7.2 (for a similar literary citation of a misguided prayer, see Hos 6.1-3). This self-confident and banal speech to Yahweh sharply contrasts with the penitent counterpart in verses 9 and 10. There we hear a chastened appellant fervently and rhetorically plead his case before a God whom he once regarded as sort of a benign benefactor, a divine guarantor of peace and prosperity, but whom he now recognizes as a righteous judge and the sovereign ruler of life and death.

Whether one considers 7.1-2 to be a continuation of 6.3 or not, it is clear that the psalm's focal contrast occurs in 7.3-4, that is, immediately after the central core, dramatizing its thematic antitype. In the experience of the psalmist, his pride certainly went before a great fall. This was a serious personal calamity that put him physically on the very brink of death and the grave (i.e., punishment [level 4], cp. stanzas A and D). But worse, it threatened to separate him spiritually from his holy God, and by implication also from fellow members of the covenant community. This conceit, a self-centered dependence on one's own resources—or assumed religious standing—was regarded as being one of the most destructive sins in Israel, whether on the personal or the national level (and hence a burden, too, of many prophetic messages). Proud self-confidence stood as a barrier to a proper acceptance of the gracious protection and provision of Yahweh. It was, in fact, the polar opposite of a complete devotion to and dependence on him, as expressed, for example, in verse 10.

At this crucial juncture, however, the psalmist's supreme crisis of body and soul is only indirectly referred to, and in the briefest, most general manner: "You-hid your-face [*reason*]; I-was dismayed [*result*]" (four words in the Hebrew, but drawn out at the end by means of a periphrastic construction). His technical skill as a poetic composer is demonstrated by the way in which he carefully positions this short poetic line in the structural nucleus of the discourse—indeed, at its very climax at the end of stanza C. Its importance is further reinforced by being placed at a point with strongly contrasting material on either side. Had these stylistic devices not been employed here, the significance of this colon, whether for the original auditors or for readers today, could have easily been missed, or at least deprived of much of its emotive impact.

Thematic implications of a concentric incorporation of linearity

There is yet another way of viewing the overall formal and topical congruence of this poem and of explaining how the several major discontinuities it contains are resolved by a larger pattern of continuity. This takes the form of an extended structural introversion consisting of paired passages that manifest a basic equivalence in their respective contents (see figure III, next page; cp. Bratcher and Reyburn 1991:282;

Lund 1930:304; Alden 1974:22-23). Most of these disjunctive parallels are characterized by semantic similarity, but several others feature some prominent contrast in their essential nature.

This integrated series of meaning correlates is another good illustration of Jakobson's poetic precept cited earlier: As the second sequence of seven (!) segments unfolds, it is simultaneously reflecting back upon itself in a progressive and systematic reiteration of corresponding elements that have already appeared in the discourse. In other words, there is a paradigmatic-syntagmatic convergence as these two fundamental principles of rhetorical composition overlap—or merge, depending on how one looks at it. The principal points of similarity or contrast are highlighted in boldfaced type on the diagram, while corresponding units are marked by the same capital letters and vertical broken lines. It is interesting to observe that the diachronic midpoint of the psalms in terms of physical mass (Hebrew accent groups) corresponds with the center of its synchronic arrangement of topical units, i.e., between [G] and [G']—44 versus 45 "words" (including the title).

Another patterned sequence, less obvious perhaps, is also manifested by the various utterances which constitute this poetic text. That is the series of shifting discourse interactions which represents the dynamic interpersonal movement of the psalm from beginning to end. As the poet joyfully but reverently engages Yahweh in thanksgiving and praise, he appears to follow a symmetrical ordering of basic illocutions, or conversational goals. In essence this consists of just two alternating elements that are linked in a cause-effect logical/semantic relationship, namely, "grounds" (***G***), or motivation, and "implication" (***I***), i.e., praise/appeal. These are shown forming a vertical string along the right-hand margin of figure III.

In other words, the psalmist cites one or more actions on the part of Yahweh that move(d) him to make a verbal rejoinder—an expression of appreciation and/or acclaim. Generally these responses are positive in nature, but as was pointed out earlier, in the center of the psalm some contrasting notions are highlighted as the poet recalls his deviation in allegiance from Yahweh to self. Thus another structural introversion of parallel elements is formed, one of a pragmatic nature that complements the semantic one outlined above. Here, too, the turning point occurs immediately after the crucial middle segment, i.e., from ***I*** → ***G*** to ***G*** → ***I*** in the middle of verse 7 (G'-F').

Figure III

A.	I-will-**exalt-you**, Yahweh, for you-lifted-me-out,	1	*I* *G*
B.	and-not-did-you-let-**rejoice** my-enemies over-me.		
C.	Yahweh, my-God, **I-cried-for-help to-you** and-**you-healed-me.**	2	
D.	Yahweh, **you-brought-up from-sheol my-soul.** You-kept-me-alive from-those-**descending-into the-pit.**	3	
E.	**Sing-praise to-Yahweh**, his-pious-ones, and-**give-thanks** for-the-memory-of his-holiness.	4	*I*
F.	For-a-moment [is] in-**his-anger**, life [is] in-his-favor. In-the-evening **it-endures weeping**, and-at-the-morning [is] a-joyous-shout.	5	*G*
G.	And-I I-said **in-my-security**, "**Not-shall-I-be-moved forever**!	6	*I*
G′	Yahweh, **in-your-favor** you-caused-[it]-to- **take-a-stand on-my-mountain** [namely] **strength**!"	7	*G*
F′	You-**hid your-face**, I-was **dismayed**!		*G*
E′	**Unto-you, Yahweh, I-will-call,** and-unto-my-Lord **I-will-plead-for-mercy.**	8	*I*
D′	What-profit [is] in-**my-blood**, in-**my-descending into-destruction**? Will-it-thank-you **the-dust**, will-it-proclaim your-faithfulness?	9	*G*
C′	**Hear**-O-Yahweh and-**show-mercy-to-me**! O-Yahweh, **be a-helper for-me**!	10	*I*
B′	You-turned my-wailing into-dancing for-me; you-removed my-sackcloth, and-you-clothed-me-with **joy**	11	*G*
A′	so-that it-may-**sing-praise-to-you** [my]-glory, and-not it-will-be-silent. Yahweh, my-God, forever I-will-thank-you!	12	*I*

It is worth noting in this connection that from an abstract perspective all psalms manifest just two basic *grounds* and two corresponding *implications* (in various combinations and proportions). Accordingly the psalmist may be motivated by either some threat or lack in his life (especially enmity and illness), or by some particular blessing from Yahweh (which often includes a deliverance from the preceding). He then makes an appropriate religious response, either a complaint (with or without an accompanying petition) or an expression of praise (which may be reinforced by a word/vow of thanksgiving or a profession of faith). Thus the two basic psalm types, *lament* and *eulogy*, are actualized in a poetic dramatization of the relationship between the faithful singer, or pray-er, and his covenant God (cp. Miller 1986:4).

Here again we have an illustration of discontinuity being swallowed up or overshadowed by continuity in literary discourse. The successive points of apparent dissimilarity or disjunction, when viewed from the perspective of the surface level of the text, are progressively incorporated within a larger and deeper framework of meaning, both expressed and implied—one which spans the entire composition. With particular reference to Psalm 30, this process of poetic fusion may be viewed as a structural metaphor that effectively mirrors the principal theme of the song. It is in essence an artistic reflection upon and extolling of the position of the Chasidim (verse 4), both in their relationship to the pressing problems of this world on the one hand, and also to their merciful and mighty Protector on the other. Thus in the battles of everyday existence, when temporal discontinuities confront the everlasting continuity of their covenant God, Yahweh is always triumphant. He in turn will eventually but most certainly deliver his pious people from the inevitable depressions of life!

A concluding thought on the "medium" of discontinuity

One more major discontinuity remains to be considered in relation to Psalm 30. It is one which, for the most part, has not yet been successfully dealt with in the communication history of this and many other biblical texts, and that is the *medium of transmission*. This subject requires a full-length study of its own, and we can simply call attention to a number of the crucial factors that need to be more thoroughly investigated in this regard.

In brief, the problem is this: a vibrant instance of religious oral literature has been fixed for the sake of ecclesiastical preservation and transmission within the primary medium of print (preceded by a long manuscript tradition). Virtually all of the psalms were either orally composed in the original instances, or they were composed (in writing) with oral presentation in mind. This fact is most clearly evidenced by the purpose and nature of the discourse itself, namely, that of a song and/or prayer encoded in the mode of direct speech. Many other features of the text testify to its essential orality; for example, its underlying rhythmic cadence (whatever this actually was in the initial event), the special accentual system, phonological effects, multileveled parallel patterns, extensive reiteration of form and content, along with many vocatives, rhetorical questions, and graphic figures of speech. Much of this gets left behind either in translation or in the reduction to writing. And as a result, the basic quality of communication gets significantly altered.

What effect, then, does this prominent discontinuity have upon the dynamics of message transmission? Obviously a considerable loss of impact and appeal is potentially involved. While it is going too far to adopt Marshall McLuhan's well-known dictum, "The medium is the message," the importance of the channel of communication does need to be strongly emphasized. Indeed, the medium *enhances* the message, depending upon the extent to which it matches the intention of the original author in this respect. His/her message suffers considerably when conveyed in a manner for which it was not originally intended. Nevertheless it is not completely destroyed or compromised, even in literary works such as the psalms, where an appreciable amount of conceptual content can survive most translations and media transpositions.

We have seen how the poet utilized a number of important stylistic techniques to harmonize or to bridge the various points of formal and semantic discontinuity in his text and to unify them within his larger patterns of discourse composition. But how can this be done in relation to the issue of media disjunction? The obvious answer is to restore the text to its original mode of presentation, namely, the oral-aural channel. But this solution does not go far enough, for we are not dealing with the original Hebrew text, but with a modern linguistic transformation of it.

Thus a version must be prepared in the receptor language that is as close as possible to a functionally equivalent rendering, that is, an artistic composition—a poetic recreation—that conveys the essential content and intent of the source message in forms that are stylistically natural—even idiomatic, if appropriate—with respect to the particular genre which has been chosen in that language (de Waard and Nida 1986: chapter 4).

Where biblical poetry is concerned, plus an audible text, even more attention and effort must be devoted to the matter of linguistic and literary form. This is to ensure the greatest degree of equivalence with respect to functional purpose across the twin barriers of language and culture. In such situations the goal is to replace one oratorical and rhetorical mode of composition with another, while preserving the fundamental constituents of cognitive [religious/theological] content (for a sample of Psalm 30 as restructured in Chitonga, see Wendland 1992).

One positive step in the direction of "re-oralizing" the biblical text in translation can possibly be taken in the area of the printed version itself. The Scriptures may be presented in a more legible and/or recitable form by means of a judicious use of typography and format design. This is especially important where a poetic passage such as a psalm is involved, because most people, no matter what their language, normally expect "poetry" (however it is defined in the RL) to manifest a distinctive style and sound. This, too, is a subject that currently demands much more consideration that it has received in the past, but the figure on the following page (figure IV) gives a sample at least of some of the features that might be included in such a venture. It is a reformatted (and slightly altered) version of the NIV translation of Psalm 30, displayed in what is hopefully a more readable—and hence also hearable—text (see Louw and Wendland 1993).

This display merely offers a suggestion as to how the sharp discontinuity with regard to both the medium of transmission and its associated manner of interpretation might be compensated for by means of a more dynamic approach in the area of graphic design (cf. the New Evangelical Translation, NET, for many good examples of such discourse-oriented formatting). The aim is to produce a version that is not only easier to read, but one which is at the same time more correctly understood in terms of its own patterns and points of meaning-significance. Does such a format help to make the original discourse structure more perceptible orally as well as visually? Does it make possible, or at least encourage, a more intelligible articulation of the text on the part of the speaker? If not, where does it fail, and what can be done to accomplish these vital objectives? And what about the vast numbers of the world's population who are unable to read? Certainly it is also time to think more seriously about preparing biblical texts specifically for oral-aural transmission in the form of "audio Scriptures" (cp. Sogaard 1991).

Is it really feasible to transform the silence of the written Word, and poetry in particular, into a more meaningful, audible "singing" in thankful praise of Yahweh (verse 13)? It is hoped that the present study might contribute to a more convincing, committed, and contextualized response to these and related issues as they pertain to the world-wide endeavor to transcend diverse discontinuities in the continued cross-cultural communication of the Scriptures.

Figure IV

Psalm 30: A song of David for the dedication of the temple

1. **I will exalt you, O LORD,**
   for you lifted me out of the depths
   and did not let my enemies gloat over me.
2. O LORD my God, I called to you for help
   and you healed me.
3. O LORD, you brought me up from the grave;
   you spared me from going down into the pit.

4. Sing to the LORD, you saints of his;
   praise his holy name.
5. For his anger lasts only a moment,
   but his favor lasts a lifetime;
   weeping may remain for a night,
   but rejoicing comes in the morning.

6. When I felt secure, I said,
   "I will never be shaken.
7. *O LORD, when you favored me,*
   you made my mountain stand firm."

BUT WHEN YOU HID YOUR FACE, I WAS DISMAYED!

8. To you, O LORD, I called;
to the Lord I cried for mercy:
9. *"What gain is there in my destruction,*
in my going down into the pit?
Will the dust praise you?
Will it proclaim your faithfulness?
10. *Hear, O LORD, and be merciful to me;*
O LORD, be my help!"

11. You turned my wailing into dancing;
you removed my sackcloth and clothed me with joy,
12. that my heart may sing to you and not be silent.
O LORD my God, I will give you thanks forever!

References

Alden, Robert L. 1974. "Chiastic Psalms: A Study in the Mechanics of Semitic Poetry in Psalms 1–50." *Journal of the Evangelical Theological Society* 17:1, pages 11-28.

Alter, Robert. 1987. "The Characteristics of Ancient Hebrew Poetry." In R. Alter and F. Kermode, editors, *The Literary Guide to the Bible*, pages 611-624. Cambridge: Harvard University Press.

Beekman, John; John Callow; and Michael Kopesec. 1981. "The Semantic Structure of Written Communication" (prepublication draft, 5th revision). Dallas: Summer Institute of Linguistics.

Bellinger, W.H. Jr. 1991. *Psalms: Reading and Studying the Book of Praises*. Peabody, MA: Hendrickson.

Berlin, Adele. 1985. *The Dynamics of Biblical Poetry*. Bloomington: Indiana University Press.

Bratcher, Robert G., and William D. Reyburn. 1991. *A Translator's Handbook on the Book of Psalms*. New York: United Bible Societies.

Craghan, John F. 1985. *The Psalms: Prayers for the Ups, Downs and In-Betweens of Life*. Wilmington, DE: Michael Glazier.

Craigie, Peter C. 1983. *Psalms 1-50* (Word Biblical Commentary). Waco, TX: Word Books.

van Gemeren, Willem A. 1991. "Psalms," in *The Expositor's Bible Commentary*, volume 5. Grand Rapids: Zondervan.

Gerstenberg, Erhard. 1988. *Psalms (Part 1) with an Introduction to Cultic Poetry* (The Forms of Old Testament Literature 14). Grand Rapids, Michigan: Eerdmans.

Jakobson, Roman. 1960. "Linguistics and Poetics," in T. Sebeok, editor, *Style in Language*, pp. 350-377. Cambridge, MA: MIT Press.

———. 1966. "Grammatical Parallelism and Its Russian Facet." *Language* 42:399-429.

———. 1987. "The Dominant." In K. Pomorska and S. Rudy, editors, *Language in Literature*, pages 41-46. Cambridge: Harvard University Press.

Leupold, D.D. 1959. *Exposition of the Psalms*. Grand Rapids: Baker.

Louw, Johannes, and Ernst Wendland. 1993. *Graphic Design and Bible Reading*. Cape Town: The Bible Society of South Africa.

Luke, Carmen. 1988. "Epistemic Rupture and Typography: 'The Archaeology of Knowledge' and 'The Order of Things' Reconsidered." *Sociolinguistics* 17/2:141-155.

Lund, Nils W. 1930. "The Presence of Chiasmus in the O.T." *The American Journal of Semitic Languages and Literatures* 46:104ff.

Miller, Patrick D., Jr. 1986. *Interpreting the Psalms.* Philadelphia: Fortress.

Nida, Eugene A. (forthcoming) "Translation: Possible *and* Impossible." Manuscript, pp. 1-13.

Oesterley, W.O.E. 1959. *The Psalms: Translated with Text-Critical and Exegetical Notes*. London: SPCK.

Perowne, J.J. Stewart. 1989. *The Book of Psalms,* vol. 1. Grand Rapids: Zondervan.

Preliminary and Interim Report on the Hebrew Old Testament Text Project [HOTTP]. Five volumes. 1973-1980. London: United Bible Societies.

Rawlinson, G. 1950. "Psalms" [Exposition], in *The Pulpit Commentary* 8. Grand Rapids: Eerdmans.

Søgaard, Viggo. 1991. *Audio Scriptures Handbook.* Reading, England: United Bible Societies.

de Waard, Jan, and Eugene Nida. 1986. *From One Language to Another: Functional Equivalence in Bible Translating*. Nashville: Thomas Nelson.

Wendland, Ernst R. 1992. "*Kulakatula Ndakatulo*—On the Translation of Biblical Poetry as Poetic Discourse in a Bantu Language." Paper presented at the AFRESCOT workshop in Nairobi, Kenya.

Zevit, Ziony. 1990. "Roman Jakobson, Psycholinguistics, and Biblical Poetry." *Journal of Biblical Literature* 109/3:385-401.

Symmetry and Prominence in Hebrew Poetry: With Examples from Hosea

Loren F. Bliese

Hebrew poetry has structural symmetry that helps to identify peaks or points of prominence. This is important for a translator to know since it shows which parts of a text need to be highlighted in the translation. Such symmetry is found both on the level of individual poems and in larger units such as the book of a prophet. For example, the book of Hosea has five parts (I: 1.1–3.5; II: 4.1–7.2; III: 7.3–8.13; IV: 8.14–11.7; and V: 11.8–14.9); the central part has five poems (7.3-7; 7.8-16; 8.1-4; 8.4-8; 8.9-13); the central poem has five lines, and the central line has five words with "my-God" the middle word 8.2, "To-me they-cry, '*My-God*, we-know-you (we-)Israel.' " This line sums up God's major accusation in the book: Israel claims to know God but is not faithful to him.

Other markers of prominence are found in this line that also help to set it off. The bad grammar of having "my" and "we" in the same sentence is particularly unique. Peak lines are more likely than nonpeak lines to have some irregularity like this. Another feature is the numerical device of having twenty-two letters in this line (the number of letters in the Hebrew alphabet), and having the first letter of God's name Yahweh as the two middle letters *yy* in the line. In fact there are significantly five *y*'s in the line, one in each of the five words in the line. The number of occurrences of this form of "God" in Hosea is twenty-two, and the number of occurrences of "Israel" is forty-four, which is a clue to the importance of these two main protagonists in the book. Multiples of twenty-two are also basic to the divisions of the book, with four of the main parts having eighty-eight lines each and each part dividing into two blocks of forty-four lines. The central part has fifty lines, which is probably a clue to the first two letters of Yahweh *yh*, which equal ten and five, and when multiplied produce fifty. Other literary devices that add to prominence will be discussed later.

In my work on Hebrew poetry, I have observed that individual Hebrew poems are of two metrical types, either chiastic with the same number of accents in corresponding lines moving from the ends toward the center, or homogeneous with all the lines of the poem having the same number of accents. These two types determine the location of the main peak of any poem. If the poem is metrically chiastic, the peak will be in the center, and if the poem is homogeneous, the peak will be at the end (see the bibliography under Bliese for detailed studies of texts). Chiastic poems are about twice as frequent. For example, Hosea has thirty chiastic poems and fifteen homogeneous poems. A nice example of a chiastic poem is Hos 2.18-20 (20-22, Hebrew):

A	18 **And-I-will-establish for-them a-covenant** **in-that day**	[3+2]	(5)
B	With=the-beasts-of the-field and-with=the-birds-of the-sky and-the-creeping-things-of the-ground.	[2+2+2]	(6)
*			
C	**And-bow and-sword and-war** **I-will-destroy from=the-earth.**	[3+2]	(5)
C′	**And-I-will-make-them-lie-down in-hope.**		
#	(enjambment)		
	19 **And-I-will-betroth-you to-me forever;**	[2+3]	(5)
B′	And-I-will-betroth-you to-me in-righteousness and-in-justice and-in-faithfulness and-in-mercy;	[2+2+2]	(6)
A′	20 **And-I-will-betroth-you to-me in-truth;** **and-you-will-know the=LORD.**	[3+2]	(5)

The chiastic symmetry of this poem is developed in several ways. First is the number of accents in each line, defined by the number of words or hyphenated units in the Masoretic Text (MT) shown in the parentheses. The first, last, and two middle lines have five accents per line, and those between them have six. This can be written in the inversion 56 55 65. The two lines in the center are the main point of prominence in such an inversion and are therefore printed in larger type. The structure of the cola in each line also balances on each side of the line. This is seen in the number of accents listed in square brackets. There are [3+2] bicola on each end in A and A′, followed by tricola [2+2+2] in B and B′. In the center the two pentameter lines match so that the longer three-accent cola are on the outside, and the shorter two-accent cola are on the inside, giving a [3+2:2+3] pattern.

The * sign near the left margin shows a strophe break. Strophes are lines that have a close connection between them. For example, A and B are one sentence about "covenant," and C and C′ have the theme of peace. Strophes usually come in couplets in Hebrew poetry. There is also a stanza break at 19 marked by #, indicating a larger thematic grouping of more than one strophe. It is posited at 19 to show the change from peace imagery to betrothal and the change from "them" to "you." In this case the stanza juncture causes an interruption of the line, technically called "enjambment." This means that the first colon of C′ connects with the previous line, and the second colon of C′ connects with the following line in forming strophes. This results in the main strophe in the peak being exceptional, with one and a half lines rather than a normal couplet. Such exceptions to the normal patterns are often found at peaks and help to give them prominence.

Another structural indicator for prominence is found when a Hebrew chiastic poem has two lines in the center rather than one. This is seen in the metrical inversion with two 5′s in the center, or in the letters CC′ in the center. Double center lines have been found to coincide with secondary emphasis at the ends, so the first and last lines in such poems have been designated as secondary peaks. They are printed in bold type to set them off. In this poem the first line has the key word "covenant," which comes significantly only once in each of the five parts of Hosea, and the words "that day" repeated from 2.16 in the previous poem. The last line has the divine name "LORD" with the key verb "know" as found in the central peak of the whole book in 8.2. It also has the third occurrence of the key phrase "And I will betroth you to me," which was introduced in the central peak in 2.19. Such repetition of divine names and other key words is one way peak lines are marked in Biblical literature. Words in the peak that are repeated elsewhere are underlined in this study to highlight their importance.

Another artfully structured chiastic poem in Hosea is 7.3-7, the first poem in the central part.

3 **By-their-evil they-delight(=)the-*king*,**
and-by-their-lies princes. [3+2] (4/5)
4 *All-of-them* are-adulterers,
as a-burning oven. [2+3] (5)
*

The-*baker* ceases from-stirring-it-up,
from-kneading the-dough until(=)it-is-leavened. [3+4] (6/7)

*

5 **On-the-day-of our-*king***
they-made the-princes-sick
from-the-heat(poison)-of the-wine [2+2+2] (6)
He-lifted(+)his-hand with=the-mockers,
6 **while=they-came-near as-an-oven,**
their-heart on-their-plots. [2+2+2] (7/6)

*

All=night their-*baker* sleeps;
in-the-morning he(+)burns like-a-flaming fire. [3+4] (8/7)

*

7 *All-of-them* are-hot as-an-oven;
and-they-devour their=rulers. [3+2] (5)
All=their-*kings* have-fallen;
none=calls from-them to-me. [2+3] (5)

If one reads this text without reference to the structure, the use of pronouns is very confusing. For example, "all of them" in 4 may refer either to the same subject as in 3 or to the "king and princes" in 3. "None of them" at the end may also refer to the "kings" or to the "all of them" in 7. However, the symmetrical arrangement of characters in the poem makes all the references clear. The first and last strophes have the assassins "all of them" first deceiving and then "devouring" their rulers, meaning "the king" and "the princes." "All of them" is to be identified then with "the mockers" in the central peak.

Similarly the second strophes from each end describe the inactivity of the "baker" until "morning," "when the dough is leavened." The middle strophe is the peak action, when the "mockers" "came near" and murdered the king. In the peak lines there is another ambiguous reference, "He lifted his hand." The immediate antecedent is the "king," so many translations have him lift his hand in innocent revelry with his mockers. However, the structure recommends identifying the "baker" as the one who "lifted his hand" to signal the assassins to kill the king (see Andersen and Freedman 1980:451-454). This will put all the participants on stage when the murder is committed, and give greater symmetry to the poem (see the "crowded stage" marker for peak described by Longacre 1983:27). The four participants come then not only in a symmetrical word chiasmus with a single reference on each side of the center, but also all four occur again in the center. This can be diagrammed as follows, and the structurally patterned words are put in italics in the text above to help see the chiasmus:

king (1st line)
 princes
  all of them as an oven (2nd line)
   baker (3rd line)
    KING, PRINCES, HIS HAND, MOCKERS AS AN OVEN
   baker (3rd line from end)
  all of them as an oven (2nd line from end)
 rulers
kings (last line).

Support for the symmetrical arrangement also comes from the consistency which this interpretation gives to the third person plural references "they/their" throughout the poem. They all refer to the "lying," "mocking" assassins. Similarly all the third person singular references, except the final one which is clearly identified as "one of them," point to the same person, "the baker." Many translations change the MT "baker" in 6 to "anger" or "passion." However, the beautiful symmetry supports keeping the MT.

The chiastic symmetry of this poem can also be seen in the metrics. The number of accents per line can be listed in the inversion 557 66 755. In this poem the symmetry is improved by deleting or adding four hyphens in the MT as shown above, with parentheses around deleted MT hyphens (=), and (+) for added hyphens. The results of the changes are indicated by the numbers after the slashes at the end of the lines. Again in this poem cola structure is symmetrical, with the exceptional tricola [2+2+2] in the two central peak lines, and the two heptameters on each side of the peak, both having the smaller colon first rather than the normal [4+3] with the larger colon first. The second and last strophes also end with an exceptional [2+3] pentameter, perhaps to further indicate disruption by the unusual amount of irregular colometry.

The center is more prose-like than the other lines; for example, note 7.3 with its parallelism. Dropping that major feature of Hebrew poetry, parallelism, is another example of the exceptional nature of peaks. The center is again a double line, which normally points to the ends for further emphasis. The final line is a didactic secondary peak climax with the lament of God, "None of them calls to me." The reference to "king/s" in both the first and last lines is an important inclusio.

Poems with Homogeneous Metrics

The second major category of metrical analysis in Hebrew poetry is poems with the same number of accents in all lines. In this type the peak is normally the last line. The function of this structure is a build-up to the end, in contrast to chiastic poems, which move from each end toward the peak in the center. A good example of a homogeneous poem is Hos 2.21-23 (23-25, Hebrew).

21 And-it-will-be in-that day
    I-will-*answer*, says=the-LORD: (5)
  I-will-*answer* the=heavens,
    and-they will-*answer* the-=*land*. (5)
*

22 And-the-*land* will-*answer* the=grain
    and-the=wine and-the=oil; (5)
  And-they will-*answer* Jezreel (or *'el*=God-*sows*);
23   and-I-will-*sow*-her(+)for-myself in-the-land. (6/5)
*

  And-I-will-have-mercy-on No Mercy;
    and-I-will-say to-Not=My-People, (5)
  "You-are(=)my-people";
    and-he will-say, "My-God." (4/5)

The number of accents in this poem is basically five. The repeated sequence builds up to the final peak, which has the key word "My-God," noted earlier as the center of the whole book in 8.2. The change of the condemnatory name "Not-My-People" to the covenant name "My-People" also gives emphasis. The build-up of a terrace pattern (Watson 1984:208-12), beginning with the word "answer" and ending with the answer of the "people" to "God," also points to the end. It shows how the metrical patterns are often duplicated by structured word repetitions. In contrast to metrically chiastic poems, where words are repeated from both ends moving toward the central peak, as seen in 7.3-7 above, in homogeneous poems the repeated words are often found in groups leading to the end.

21 answer answer answer
21-22 land land
22 answer answer
22-23 sow-God sow (23 land)
23 mercy mercy
23 not not
23 people people God

Another example of a homogeneous poem with a terrace pattern leading to the final climax is Hos 5.12–6.3. The poem also has emphasis at the end of the first stanza, 14b and its following line, which are the center of the poem. It has twelve hexameters as follows:

12 And-*I*-am like-a-moth to-*Ephraim*,
and-like-rot to-the-house of-*Judah*; (6)
*
13 And-*Ephraim* saw his=sickness,
and-*Judah* his(=)wound; (5/6)
Then-*Ephraim* went *to*=Assyria,
and-he-sent *to*=the-great king; (6)
But-he was-*not*(+)able to-*heal*(+)you;
and-he-did-*not*=cure *your* wound; (8/6)
*
14 For(+)I-am like-a-lion *to-Ephraim*,
and-like-a-young-lion *to*-the-house of-*Judah*; (7/6)
I, I will-*tear and-will-go*;
I-will-carry-away, and-no-one(+)will-rescue. [4+2] (7/6)

#
15 I-*will-go*, I-will-*return* to=my-place,
until they=admit-their-guilt, and-seek(+)my-face; (7/6)
*
In-their troubles they-will-seek-me:
1 "Come, and-let's-*return* to=the-LORD, (6)
For he has-*torn*, but-he-will-*heal-us*;
he-has-hit, but-he-will-bandage-*us*. [4+2] (6)
2 After-two-*days* he-will-*revive-us*,
on-the-third(+) *day* he-will-raise-us-up;
that-we-may-*live* before-him. [2+2+2] (7/6)

*

3 **So-let's-know,** (1) (anacrusis)
Let's-press-on to-know the=LORD,
like -the- dawn his-going-forth is-sure; (6)
And-he-comes to-us like-showers,
like-spring-rains that-water the-earth." (6)

This poem has overall unity in similes about God: "moth" and "rot" in the first line, "lion" and "young lion" in the middle, and "dawn," "showers," and "spring rains" at the end. The last peak line has inverted parallelism, with the similes in the center and the verbs "comes" and "water" outside. The penultimate line, which here is counted as part of the peak, also has inverted parallelism, with two verbals followed by the noun "LORD," and the noun "dawn" followed by two verbs. Anacrusis, "So let's know," sets off the final two lines as the peak, with the thematic word "know" repeated in "know the LORD."

A terrace pattern helps to point to the final peak, with God's expressed desire that his people turn to know him so his judgment may turn to blessing:

like(moth), like(rot) (12)
Ephraim, Judah (12)-Ephraim, Judah (13a)-Ephraim (13b)
to-to(13b)
not, you-not, you (13c)
like(lion) to Ephraim, like(young lion), to Judah (14)
I-I (14b) (also 12 and variant in 14)
go (14b)-go (15a)
return, to (15a)-return, to (1a)
-us - -us (1b)
revive-us – live (2a)
day-day (2a)
KNOW-KNOW (THE LORD) (3a)
LIKE- (3a) LIKE- LIKE- (3b).

The final peak also has emphasis by synonyms, with the first "as dawn" referring back to "day" in 3, and the last two phrases being "as showers" and "as spring rains that water the earth." The agricultural simile for God also relates to the last major poem in 14.5ff., "I will be as dew to Israel . . . ."

The two halves of the poem are also structurally symmetrical. The first stanza (12-14) has the emphatic pronoun "I" as the first word, and the last line 14b has it repeated twice. The first six roots of this last line all begin with *'alef*, marking it as the climax of the stanza.

The second stanza is the same length, with six hexameters. It also has the same strophic structure, with a single bicolon where God describes his activities, followed by a three-line strophe and a final two-line strophe. This structure suggests that the words of Israel in 1-3 are what God expects them to say when they return, and should not be taken as true repentance at this stage in the book. The name "LORD" comes in the second line from each end of this stanza (the only occurrences in the poem). The Hebrew for "seek" in the first line (15) has the same root as "dawn" in the next to the last line. The first word "Go," speaking of God's departure, is reversed with the first word of the last line, "come."

Some word chiasmus gives cohesion to the whole poem and may give emphasis to God's action in judgment in the center (the climax of the first stanza and beginning of the second). This can be seen in that the two stanzas are tied together by anadiplosis, "I will go," in the middle lines on each side of the junctures, and by the word "tear" in the end of the first stanza and the middle of the second. Furthermore, the word "heal" is in the fourth line from each end, first negatively of Assyria, then positively of God.

Secondary Peaks

Hebrew poetry has other distinguishable ways to give prominence to lines other than the center of a chiasmus or the end of a homogeneous series. Some of these are particularly tied to structure. For example, in the two chiastic poems discussed above from Hos 2.18-20 (20-22) and 7.3-7, it was noted that a double line in the center is a pointer to prominence in the first and last lines as well as in the center. In my studies I have called them secondary peaks, since the prominence on the average is statistically greater than on nonpeak lines but is less than in the major peak of each poem. In translation, receptor language variations of marking prominence can possibly be considered in giving primary emphasis at peaks and secondary emphasis at these other places.

Another structural pointer to prominence in chiastic poems is length that exceeds eighteen lines. In some cases even seventeen-line poems have been candidates for the same type of prominence, so the number of lines is only suggested here as the length most clearly illustrating this structure in Hosea. The point of secondary prominence in such long poems is at the quarter points, with the main peak in the chiastic center of the poem. A good example is Hos 9.1-9, one of three nineteen-line poems in Hosea with the same structure (see 2.2-8 and 7.8-16).

1 Don't=rejoice, Israel,
unto=exalting like-the-nations; (4)
For you-have-played-the-harlot,
leaving your-*God*. (4)
You-have-loved harlot's-wages
on all=threshing-floors-of grain. [2+3] (5)
*
2 Threshing-floor and-winepress will-not(+)feed-them,
and-new-wine will-fail(+)in-her. (7/5)
3 **They-will-not live**
in-the-land of-the-LORD; (quarter line) (4)
But-Ephraim will-return to-Egypt,
and-in-Assyria they-will-eat(+)unclean-food. (6/5)
*
4 They-will-not=pour-out wine to-the-LORD,
nor please=him with-their-sacrifices; (6)
It-will-be-for-them as-bread-of mourning;
all(=)who-eat-it will-be-polluted. (5/6)
For=their-bread is-for-their-throat;
it-will-not enter the-house-of the-LORD; [2+4] (6)
*
5 **What=will-you-do for-the-day-of the-festival,**
and-for-the-day-of the-feast-of=the-LORD? (5)
#
6 Yes,=behold, (1) (anacrusis)
They-went-away from-destruction;
Egypt will-gather-them;
Memphis will-bury-them. [2+2+2] (6)
Their-precious-things of-silver,
nettles will-possess,
thorns-will-be in-their-tents. [2+2+2] (6)

7 The-days-of(+)punishment have-come;
the-days-of(+)paying-up have-come;
let-Israel know! [2+2+2] (8/6)

*

"The-*prophet* is-a-fool,
the-man-of the-spirit is-mad," [2+3] (5)
Because-of(+)your-*great iniquity*,
and-*great hostility*. (quarter line) (5/4)

*

8 He-is-the-watchman-of Ephraim,
the-*prophet* with(=)my-God. [2+3] (4/5)
There-is-a-fowler's snare on=all=his-ways;
hostility in-the-house-of(+)his-*God*. (6/5)

*

9 They-became-deeply(=)corrupted
as-in-the-days-of Gibeah; (3/4)
He-will-remember their-*iniquity*;
he-will-punish their-sins. (4)

First a look at the overall chiastic pattern will help to get a feel for the whole poem. A metrical inversion of 445545666 5 (1)666545544 is proposed for this chiasmus. The extra (1) beginning 9.6 is called anacrusis, an extra accent unit beginning a new section. The lines on each side of the center both have irregular cola structure. There is also balance with "God" (1b) and "land of the LORD" (3a) in the first half, and "God" (8a) and "house of his God" (8b) in the second half, although in this case not coming in lines the same distance from the center as is often the case.

The central peak of 9.5 in this poem is a single line. It is marked by the "abrupt change to second-person plural in this verse, the only occurrence of that person and number . . ." (Andersen and Freedman 1980:529). The peak also has the divine name "LORD," which is repeated from 3a, 4a, and 4c in a build-up to the peak. It also has rhetorical questions to set it off. "Day" comes twice in the peak and near the end in 9, illustrating the feature of repetition both within peak and of peak words repeated elsewhere in the poem. Strophic structure also sets off the single peak line, which stands in a strophe of its own.

The structural pattern pointing to the quarter lines can be found by counting to the fifth line from each end. The center (3a) of the first half is the strong thematic condemnation, "not live in the land of the LORD."

The first stanza has a semantic pattern of chiasmus, with the secondary peak "land of the LORD" at the center as follows:

A rejoice . . . exalt 1a — A′ festival . . . feast 5
B God 1b — B′ LORD 4c
C grain 1c — C′ bread 4b,c
D new wine 2 — D′ wine 4a
E land of LORD 3a — E′ Egypt . . . Assyria 3b.

The quarter line in the second half of the poem is the last line of 9.7. The cola on each side of this line set it off by both having the exceptional pattern of [2+3] and the word "prophet" in common. The repetition of "great" in this line and of "hostility" in 8b, and "iniquity" in 9b as well as 7, is typical of peak lines. The whole line is a prepositional phrase "because of," illustrating syntactic complexity, which is also a common marker of peak. This secondary peak is set off by being the only second person singular reference in the stanza. It relates to the first lines of the poem with the same second person singular. A significant chiastic sequence with words in each colon of this line and its two adjacent lines highlights this secondary peak:

A prophet — A′ prophet
B man of the spirit — B′ watchman
C great iniquity — C′ great hostility.

We will also take a look at the longest poem in Hosea, 13.12–14.8(9), for secondary peak patterns. This is thematically one of the most important in the book and is a good example of Hebrew poetic structures. The poem illustrates three types of secondary peaks that are important to note in analyses of prominence in Hebrew poetry: (1) the central peak has two lines, a structure which points to the first and last lines for prominence; (2) the poem is long, so the quarter lines have prominence; and (3) there are several monocolon lines, which, because of their shortness and terse nature, have consistently been found to qualify for prominence in Hebrew poetry. The monocola in this poem are of both bimeter and trimeter length. Significantly most of them come adjacent either to the central peak or to the long secondary peaks at the quarters, which helps to set these lines off by the contrast in length. The metrical chiasmus of 13.12–14.8(9) shows this pattern: 5755637445542 77 2455(3)447365575. The poem divides into two parts, with the juncture just before the central peak—chapter thirteen deals with judgment and punishment, and chapter fourteen with salvation and blessing. Since these themes are opposite, they are traditionally not put together in one poem when translated. However, the build-up of these two major themes to this last poem in the book before the final short wisdom poem makes a strong appeal by combining them in this longest climax.

12 **Bound-up is-the-iniquity of-*Ephraim*;**
stored-up is-his-sin. (secondary peak) (5)

*

13 Pangs-of birth come to-him;
he-is=a-son without wisdom. (7)
For=at-the-time he-does-not(=)stand
at-the-breaking(forth) of-children. (4/5)

*

14 Shall-I-ransom-them from-the-hand-of Sheol?
Shall-I-redeem-them from-death? (5)
I-will-be[Where-are] your-plagues, Death!
I-will-be[Where-is] your-destruction, Sheol! (6)
Compassion is-hidden from-my-eyes. (secondary peak) (3)

#

15 **Though he-be a-son-of his-brothers bearing-fruit,**
the-east-wind will-come; (secondary peak) [5+2] (7)
The-wind-of the-LORD
will-arise from-the-desert, (4)
And-his-fountain will-dry-up,
and-his-spring will-go-dry. (4)

*

He will-strip the-treasury
of-all=things precious. (5)
16 Samaria will-bear-her-guilt
because she-rebelled against-her-God. [2+3] (5)

*

They-will-fall by-the-sword;
their-babies will-be-dashed-to-pieces, (4)
And-his-pregnant-women will-be-split-open. (secondary peak) (2)

#

1 **Return, Israel,**
to(+)the-LORD your-God,
for you-have-stumbled in-your-iniquity;
(central peak) [2+2+3] (8/7)

*

2 **Take words with-you,**
and-return to=the-LORD;
say to-him: [3+2+2] (7)

*

"Forgive all=iniquity. (secondary peak) (2)
Accept=good, and-we-will-pay
the-bulls[fruits] of-our-lips. (4)
*
3 Assyria will-not save-us,
we(+)won't-ride on=horses; (6/5)
And-we-won't=say again, 'Our-God'
to-the-work-of our-hands; (5)
It-is=in-you that-the-orphan finds-mercy." (3 extra)
(secondary peak)
4 I-will-heal their-back-sliding (turning);
I-will-love-them freely, (4)
For my-anger
returned from-him. (4)
*
5 **I-will-be as-dew to-Israel;**
he-will-blossom as-a-lily,
and-strike his-roots. (secondary peak) [3+2+2] (7)
6 **As-Lebanon his-shoots will-sprout,** (secondary peak) (3)
And-his-beauty will-be as-the-olive,
and-he-will-have fragrance as-Lebanon. (6)
*
7 They-will-return dwelling in-his(my)-shadow;
they-will-grow grain; (5)
And-they-will-blossom as-a-vine;
his-remembrance-will-be as-wine-of Lebanon. [2+3] (5)
*
8 Ephraim, what still=do-I[he]-have-to-do with-idols?
I answer and-look-after-him. (7)
I am-like-a-green cypress;
it-is-from-me that-your-*fruit*(+)is-found.
(secondary peak) (6/5)

The central peak of this longest twenty-nine-line poem in Hosea is marked by being a heptameter tricola couplet with chiastically structured cola 2+2+3; 3+2+2. In this analysis it is set off by two-foot lines on each side, although thematically 16c can be considered the continuation of 16b, as in *Biblia Hebraice Stuttgartensia* (BHS). The proposed contrast is significant, since heptameters are the longest and bimeters the shortest lines in the book of Hosea. The divine names "LORD your-God" come in the exact center of the first line of the peak, and "LORD" also comes in the central colon of the second line of the peak. The root of "return" occurs in each line of the central peak, with a total of five times in 1-7(2-8) (Yee 1987:133), and twenty-two times in the whole book. As was noted in regard to the central peak of the book in 8.2, "Israel," the second word of this major peak, occurs forty-four times in the book, and "God" in the construct form occurs twenty-two times (Andersen and Forbes 1989:338, 276). There is a repeated parallel sequence extending into the next short secondary peak line: "return-to the LORD-iniquity; return-to the LORD-iniquity." "Iniquity" is also in the first line of the poem. The four imperatives "return, take, return, say" give special emphasis in the peak. "Take" in the peak and "accept" with the same root in the second line after the peak recall the second word of the first command of God to Hosea in 1.2, which is the second and shortest poem in Hosea, in contrast to this second from the end and longest poem.

"Ephraim" comes in the first line and again as a vocative climax in the second line from the end, the first line of the last strophe. "Ephraim" also has its root meaning "fruit" repeated in the last line, where it is connected to the thematic concept of God as the source, "It is from me that your fruit is found." Since the center is a couplet, secondary peaks are to be expected at the ends, making the occurrence of this theme in these lines significant. The first line is also set off as the only single-line strophe in the poem. Also in the first line the words "bound-up" and "stored" are significant as an old Canaanite (Ugaritic) word pair.

Besides the "Ephraim . . . fruit" inclusio, other overall chiastic correspondences point to the center. "Ransom from Sheol" and "redeem from death" (14) in the fourth line correspond antithetically to "grow" (7), literally "make live," in the fourth from the end. "God" occurs in the eleventh lines (16, 3). The repetition of "return" and the "LORD-God-LORD" sequence in the central peak was noted above, filling in this semantic chiasmus.

Quarter-lines in long poems have been counted as secondary peaks. Note that these lines are also long, heptameter, like the central peak. The seventh line (15) is the midline of the first half of the poem. It has another occurrence of "fruit," as noted in the secondary peak inclusio with "Ephraim." The plant references in 14.5 reinforce the same theme in the middle of the second half, especially "blossom," which has the same */pr/* sequence as "Ephraim" and "fruit." "Blossom" is also repeated in 7, giving emphasis. The contrast between the dry "east wind" of the midpoint (15) in the first half, and "dew" in the midpoint (5) in the second half, points out the basic shift from judgment to salvation. The secondary peak in the middle line of the second half significantly has the final twenty-second occurrence of "Israel" in the book.

Monocolon lines are also counted as secondary peaks. The trimeter line in 14.6 continues the plant imagery. "Lebanon" here is repeated in the next line, giving emphasis to this symbol of botanical abundance. In the first half of the poem, the trimeter at the end of 13.14 significantly clarifies the ambiguous references to "Sheol" and "Death" in the preceding rhetorical question by stating that "Compassion is hidden from my eyes." The synonyms in the trimeters ending the first and third stanzas, "compassion" (13.14) and "mercy," (14.3), both have the same final two consonants, giving further cohesion between the halves.

The monocolon trimeter in 14.3 stands outside of the metrical chiasmus. The function of this extra line goes beyond closure of the stanza. It is also the closure of the model prayer of repentance given to Israel in 14.2-3. The word "mercy" relates back to the prophetic name "(No) Mercy" at the beginning of the book, and "orphan" relates to "(Not) My People." The only hope for orphaned Israel is in God, who has "mercy." The extra line has special emphasis by coming outside the regular chiastic structure. It has two *y*'s, which is the first letter of Yahweh, and these *y*'s may cryptically emphasize that the "you" is Yahweh, as was done in the central peak of the book in 8.2. The two *y*'s may also be a device related to the irregular placement of this line, since it is the twentieth line from the beginning of the poem. The numerical equivalent of *y* is ten, with the two tens suggesting a correspondence with the exceptional twentieth line. Note the similar extra lines in Hosea's chiastic poems: the first in 7.1c, the tenth line of the poem, with one *y* in the line near the end of block 4; and the other in 9.16a, the fifteenth line of the poem, with one *y* and two *h*'s (which has the value of five) near the end of block six. The final extra line in 14.3c seems to be the climax of a buildup (10, 15, 20) of these exceptionally placed lines, "It is in you that the orphan finds mercy!"

There are also two monocolon bimeters in this long poem, one on each side of the center peak. The first one is the final statement of judgment, "And his pregnant women will be split open," predicting the greatest war atrocity against Israel. The other is the beginning of the model prayer introduced in the central peak, "Forgive all iniquity." The key word "iniquity" was noted to be also in the secondary peak 12, which is the first line of the poem, and at the end of the first line of the central peak.

Features That Characterize Peaks

Several features that give prominence to peak lines have been mentioned above, such as divine names, repeated key words, exceptional grammar, and dropping the normal poetic features of parallelism, bicolon lines, and couplet strophes. Longacre (1983:28-32) has especially noted the change from normal patterns as characteristic of peaks in literature. In order to substantiate the claim that peak lines are different from nonpeak lines, the occurrences of various literary features in relation to peak, secondary peak, and nonpeak lines in the book of Hosea have been counted. The percentages of occurrences in each of these three types of lines have been compared, and the probability of the differences being nonchance has been calculated statistically by chi-square. The .10 figures are normally interpreted as having only a 90% probability but do indicate interesting data. The .05 figures show a significant 95% probability and the highest .005 figures show over 99% probability. The number of peak lines is 60, and the number of secondary peak lines is 64, of which 33 are full lines (not monocola), leaving 278 nonpeak lines. The percentages are calculated by dividing the number of occurrences in each type of lines by the number of lines in that type (or full lines, if the shortness of secondary peak monocola has excluded occurrences). For details and lists of occurrences of each literary feature, see the 1993 revision of my "Metrical Chiasmus, Peak and Structural Symmetry in Hosea"(Bliese 1982).

Features in Peak	**%-of-Occurrences**			**Probability**
	Peak	**Sec.**	**Non.**	
Divine Names (LORD or God)	46.6	17.2	11.9	.005
Regular Bicola Structure (calculated by irregular lines less juncture and balance)	4.2	6.1	13.8	.025
Unique Line Length in Poem	18.3	10.9	.7	.005
Single Line Strophes	13.3	9.4	3.2	.025
Switches to 2nd Person	10.0	9.4	3.6	.10
Imperatives (less poem openers)	15.0	4.7	4.0	.01
Dropping Semantic Parallelism	20.0	12.5	4.7	.005
Avoiding Syntactic Parallelism (calculated by those with it)	5.0	6.1	14.4	.025
Avoiding Word Pair Parallelism (calculated by those with it)	20.0	27.3	37.4	.05

Features with Only Two Types Calculated for Chi-square:

1. Features with Secondary Lower than Non-peak:	**%-of-Occurrences**			**Probability**
	Peak	**Sec.**	**Non.**	
Repetition within Lines	11.7	(1.6)	5.0	.05
Syntactic Chiasmus in Lines (less those at juncture)	15.0	(6.1)	6.8	.05
Switches Plural to Singular	16.7	(4.7)	8.3	.05
Switches of Number for the same Referent within a Line	11.7	(0.0)	1.8	.005
Enjambment	7.5	(0.0)	2.3	.10
ki Syntactic Complexity	25.0	(12.5)	15.1	.10
Avoiding Number Switch Parall. (calculated by those with it)	5.0	(2.9)	11.2	.10
2. When Secondary Peak Figures Are Too Close to Another:				
Lists of Three or More	11.7	(9.1)	5.4	.10
22 Letters per Line (less at juncture and before peaks)	8.3	(6.1)	3.0	.10
Anacrusis (less poem openers)	3.3	(3.0)	0.4	.10

The weight of these figures gives very strong support to the hypothesis that structure can be used to define peak in Biblical poetry. The details of the structural analysis also receive confirmation by these figures, namely, that (1) metrically chiastic poems have a peak in the center, and (2) metrically homogeneous poems have a peak at the end, and that (3) secondary peaks can be defined on the basis of (a) first and last lines of chiastic poems with a double line in the center, (b) quarter lines of long chiastic poems, and (c) all monocola.

The occurrences of divine names in peak lines is the most striking. This has also been calculated for Joel with an even greater gap, occurring more than four times more frequently in peaks than nonpeaks (Bliese 1988a:76-77; also see Bliese 1990:268, 271, 273, 276ff. on Psalms 1–24). Shoshany (1986:190-200) includes divine references as a marker of strong lines, and Youngblood (1989:174ff.) notes the occurrences of divine names in the center of many Psalms.

It is important to note that parallelism in its various forms is often avoided or dropped at peak. Parallelism is generally recognized as the essential feature of Hebrew poetry (Kugel 1981 and Alter 1985). The decrease in peaks corroborates discourse analysis studies which have noted that peak lines leave the normal patterns. It does not mean that no peak lines have parallelism (see 9.5 above). In fact some have more carefully worked parallelism than the rest of the poem (see Hos 9.14b, "Give them a womb that miscarries, and breasts that are dry"). There are also two basically homogeneous poems in Hosea which have identical structures, with parallelism in three consecutive hexameter lines, then a monocolon secondary peak breaking the pattern, and a final hexameter with especially well-formed parallelism (see 11.12–12.1 [12.1-2, Hebrew] in Bliese 1982, and 6.4-6 below). Here the resumption of parallelism in the final line after the break is a significant marker in conjunction with the secondary peak without it:

4 What shall-I-do=with-you, Ephraim?
 What shall-I-do=with-you, Judah? (6)
Your-<u>faithfulness</u> is-like-a-morning(=)cloud,
 and-like-dew which-goes-away early. (5/6)

*

5 There=fore I-cut-them-in-pieces by-the-prophets;
 I-killed-them by-the-words-of(=)my-mouth; (5/6)
And-your[my]-judgment goes-forth like-light. (3)

*

6 **For(+)I-desire <u>faithfulness</u>, and-not=sacrifice;**
 And-knowledge of-God more-than-burnt-offerings. (7/6)

In spite of such exceptions, the overall counts show significantly less parallelism of various kinds in peak lines than in either secondary peaks or nonpeak lines. The Hosea analysis included other types of parallelism which were not statistically significant, but which all showed less parallelism in peak lines than nonpeak. Rhyme was counted when consecutive cola had the same sound. Rhyme was found in 15% of peak, 11.8% of secondary, and 21.7% of nonpeak lines. Gender switch as a form of parallelism was nearly the same in all categories: peak 8.3%, secondary 6.1%, and nonpeak 9%. Positive-negative contrast or antithetical parallelism came to 6.7% in peak, 6.1% in secondary, and 7.6% in nonpeak.

The greater number of regular bicola in peak lines seems to contradict the principle that peak lines are exceptional to the norm. The overall figures for the number of irregular cola were not statistically significant, with 17.5% in peak lines, 15.2% in secondary peaks, and 24.3% in nonpeak lines. However, because the figures suggest a tendency, the lines which produce balance or mark juncture by their irregularity were subtracted, giving the results in the above chart. The situation in Hosea then seems to be that, after the removal of irregular lines which create overall balance and those which mark juncture, the remainder show a greater preference for well-formed bicola in peak lines as compared to nonpeak lines.

The greater use of syntactic chiasmus or inverted parallelism in peak lines is also not statistically significant when all occurrences are calculated. The nonpeak percentage is 10.4% if the ten references with juncture are not subtracted. However, this figure is notably smaller than the 15% in peak, thereby suggesting a preference for chiasmus in peak. The removal of the juncture examples, as was done in the above chart, gives a sufficient difference to show a 95% probability of nonchance. This seems likely, since chiasmus in general has been shown to mark peak in Hebrew poetry—by both overall metrical chiasmus and semantic repetition leading to the central peak. Chiasmus within a single line then has the same function. It requires special attention to create, and marks those lines which have an inversion. It can be noted that the inversion often produces word order arrangements that would not be normal, so in the grammatical sense the lines are exceptional. The examples in Hosea where line chiasmus occurred were further analyzed, showing that peak lines have a significantly higher percentage of inversions that are well formed in the sense of not only parts of speech but also grammatical categories being paired. If only these are calculated, peak lines have 13.3% and nonpeak 7.2%, which gives a 90% probability of nonchance without subtracting the juncture references. The occurrences found are listed below according to their type, with V for verb, P for prepositional phrase, S for subject, O for object, and 1 for root identity. The root is identified in quotation marks.

Peak Line Chiasmus

V S1S1 V 1.11 "children."
O V1V1 O 4.6 "reject."
OVVO 4.10-11; 5.6 (although both verbs in 1st colon).
V P1P1 V 6.3b "as."
P1 VV P1 7.12b "as."
PVVP (7.14b secondary peak).

VOOV 13.2.
P1 SS P1 10.5 "on it."
VSPV (7.2 secondary peak).
V Infinitive O; P Participle Verbal 6.3a.

Note that the first nine examples (eight in peak and one in secondary peak) have two pairs of the same grammatical categories arranged chiastically. This shows special care in the formation of chiasmus in peak lines. Chiasmus in peaks which extends beyond one line was also noted in 1.6-7; 8.14; (9.7b-8a).

Nonpeak Line Chiasmus
[Those at juncture in brackets]

[VOOV 2.6b (opens stanza); 4.9b (begins poem).]
VSSV 4.13c; 10.14c
S V1V1 S 8.7c-8 "swallow."
[S1 VV S1 4.4a "man" (ends poem).]
[SVVS 6.1b (3rd line from final peak, all with chiasmus)]; 10.6B 11,10B.
PVVP 10.10a.
V P1P1 V 12.2b "as."
VPPV 9.3b; 12.12b; 13.3.
PSSP 14.6b.
[P P1P1 P 13.7 "as" (begins poem).]
VOSV 5.3; 10.3B.
[VPOV 7.2 (2nd line before peak ending 4th block).]
VOPV 8.1B (line before central peak of book); 8.12.
OVVP 12.6B
[P V1V1 O 13.6 "full" (last full line).]
P Adjective1 V1 S 4.16 "stubborn."
Pronoun1 S Complement Pron1 8.6A "he" (before peak).
[Conjunction S Verbal Verbal S P 13.1 (last full line).]

Tricola Lines
[VP, PV, VP 6.2 (line before final couplet peak).]
VO, OV, VO 10.13.
[VP, SOV, PV 12.10A (begins stanza).]

Note that the first ten and last four types have at least two pairs of the same categories paired chiastically. There are twenty such especially well-formed examples, giving a smaller ratio than those of peak lines.

The feature of repetition should be noted as being enhanced in peak, in contrast to Shoshany (1986:171ff.), who lists it as a marker of "weak" lines. The figures in Hosea confirm Longacre (1983:26), who notes that "rhetorical underlining" with "extra words" is a feature of peak. Besides repetitions within the peak lines that are calculated above, repetitions between peak lines and other lines in the same poem are also significant. As noted in the texts above, the repeated words help to direct the hearer to either the final line if repeated in a terrace pattern, or to the center if repeated in an inversion. Often the terrace repetitions also have the last repetition of several words in the final peak. This results in an inclusio when the first word of the terrace is near the beginning of the poem. Inclusio is also common in chiastic repetition, so its presence does not predict the type of word patterning pointing out peak. An example comes in Hos 11.5-7, a homogeneous poem with five pentameters.

5 Shall-he-not return
  to(=)the-land-of Egypt? [2+3] (4/5)
But-Assyria is his-king,
  because(+)they-refused to-return. (6/5)

*

6 So-the-sword will-whirl-through his-cities,
  and-finish his-bars[idle talk], (5)
And-eat their-advice.

* (enjambment)

7 **But-my-people are-bent on-turning-from-me;** [2+3] (5)
So-to=the-yoke [or MT "**up**"] **they-called-him;**
  no one will-lift-them-up. [2+3] (5)

This poem has its first three words repeated in the final peak, "not return to." The other end of the inclusio has each word separately in one of the three cola of the peak, in the order "turning, to, no." "Return/turn" is repeated three times in the poem, each with a different meaning, namely (1) go back, (2) repent, and (3) go away from. The repetition suggests a terrace pattern pointing to a final climax. The climax then begins with the half-line after the enjambment, "But my people are bent on turning from me." Another type of inclusio is the rhetorical question in the first line which is answered in the last line, verifying the exile. The next poem has the same feature with a rhetorical question in

11.8, "How can I give you up, Ephraim, and hand you over, Israel?" answered in the last line 11.11b, "And I will return them to their homes, says the LORD." The key word "return," which is repeated near the end of these consecutive poems (epiphora), now has a fourth meaning, "bring back." This build-up is significant, as is the reversal from the surety of exile in 11.5-7 to the surety of "return" from exile in 11.8-11. These two poems are on each side of the boundary of the final part V in Hosea, and mark the thematic change from pure judgment poems to a return to some salvation poems as in part I. The idea of "lifting" is also emphasized by coming at the end of 11.7 and the previous poem (epiphora in the other direction).

Besides the terrace pattern and inclusio, the final peak is marked by a grammatical inversion, plural-singular; singular-plural of subjects and objects: "they called-*him*; no one will lift-*them*." This is particularly interesting, since the pronouns thereby reverse number in each colon. This also resembles the previous peak in 11.3, "But I made Ephraim walk, taking *them* on *his* arms." In Hosea this kind of switch in number for the same referent within a line is one of the strongest markers of peak, with over 99% probability of nonchance, as noted in the above table. The fourth line has enjambment recalling many of the earlier poems in Hosea. There are three strophes. The enjambment causes the second and third to be a half-line short of a regular couplet, a device which also sets off the final peak. There are three repetitions of number switches for "people," with a pattern of singular-singular-plural coming once in each strophe. This grammatical terrace pattern therefore parallels the terrace of "return" and supports including the whole last strophe (all of 11.7) as the peak, with the final occurrence of "turn" and the key word "my people" in 7a.

Strophe 1	not he-return	to	his		they return	(5)
Strophe 2	his		his		their	(6)
Strophe 3	MY PEOPLE TURN	TO	HIM	NOT	THEM	(7)

Another literary feature which has a higher percentage for peaks is metaphor. However, the figures are too close to give statistical verification. Peak lines have 6.7%, secondary 4.4%, and nonpeak 4.0%. The figures for similes is peak 16.7%, secondary 17.6%, and nonpeak 18.4%. The use of these figures of speech should therefore be considered a general feature without a significant difference in peak.

Rhetorical questions have a high degree of association with peak in Joel (Bliese 1988a:79-80) and Nahum (Bliese 1993a). However, in Hosea peak has only 3.3%, while nonpeak has 5.0%, with none in secondary.

Specific literary features are characteristic of individual authors, so care must be taken not to generalize from one author to another in text analysis.

Translating Peak and Chiasmus

The structural and grammatical features that mark peak in Hebrew should not be ignored in translation. Cotterell and Turner (1989:195) note, "If everything is *equally* stressed, little if anything is communicated." Obviously the same features cannot be reproduced one-for-one in a different language. The important thing for a translator to realize is that Hebrew has many ways to point out what the author wanted to emphasize. Some of these, such as repetition of the same word or root in the same line or strophe, work nicely, for example, in many Ethiopian languages (see Bliese 1991c), but in many other languages these would be considered bad style rather than good. The feature of "rhetorical underlining" or using "extra words" and "tautologies" at peak (Longacre 1983:26) is probably a universal of the grammar of discourse, but the question of whether to repeat the same word, as in Hebrew, or to choose synonyms, is language specific.

Hebrew sound devices such as alliteration—either consonance where words in a sequence have the same consonant, or assonance where they have the same vowel—may be recognized markers if the translation is done in poetry. But alliteration may also seem like a tongue-twisting game rather than a way to mark something important. The principle, however, is relevant, that peak lines are likely to have more care in bringing out striking sound patterns. Rhyme, although not a required feature in Hebrew, may be one of the most widely used markers of elevated style. For example, sermon outlines with headings that rhyme with each other are considered good style in English.

Number and gender switches are likely to be confusing rather than pleasing, since they sometimes give different grammatical markers for the same thing in Hebrew. However, the principle of exceptional grammar and unusual features that call attention to the peak line is valid in any language. Change of pace, which is shown in Hebrew by more or fewer syllables in the accent units, the exceptional length of peak lines, or departure from couplet strophes at peak, is another place to expect a discourse universal. The metrical system of the receiver language will determine how pace is changed.

It has been shown that parallelism is a regular feature of Hebrew poetry, and therefore decreases at peak in order to show exceptional style. However, parallel syntactic structures are common for marking high points in many languages, including Hebrew. The important thing for the translator is to analyze his own language to find what the general features of the receptor language poetry are, and then to see whether they are decreased at peaks. This will help to identify what markers of peak are used by good poets. The function of the Ḥebrew form may then be replaced by an entirely different form which does the same thing—mark peak.

Chiasmus is obviously one of the most difficult things to deal with in translation. The simplest form is the arrangement of parts of speech in adjoining clauses so that they come in an ABB′A′ or similar inversion. This is easy to do in some languages with free word order—but the question is, "Does it mark something important?" If the function is not recognized, there is no point in it, and another marker should be found. Another form of chiasmus is the listing of words or synonyms in mirror image, usually meeting in the central peak. Since Bible translators generally try to stay close to the order of the original sequences, the result will often be similar. It is useful to have first recognized which key words are repeated in the original language, so that they may also be repeated in the translation. However, one should never sacrifice meaning or collocation in the translation in an effort to repeat key words. The point then is "Will this chiastic inversion of a series of words be recognized as pointing to the peak, or not?" If not, it may be useful to use italics or bold print to mark them, as I have done in these Hosea texts. The use of printing style to mark text is already done to some extent in choosing prose or poetry format. The use of bold print in section headings is also common and could well be added to peak lines and emphatic words in the text (see Bliese 1988b:215). Another less effective help would be to add a note explaining the function of the repeated words. Chiastic relationships between stanzas in a poem can often be shown by section headings tagged with A B C B′ A′ etc. Longer chiastic structures such as in a block, or even a book, should be noted in the introductions.

Metrical chiasmus is likely to be the most difficult to translate in its function of marking peak. No translation will show whether the original poem was chiastic or homogeneous, a feature which this paper describes as essential to knowing whether to expect the central or the final line as the peak line in each poem. Language typology shows that verb-final languages prefer to have a build-up to the main point at the final climax. This makes the translation of homogeneous poems easier in these languages. The effective translation of chiastic poems, however, may require a massive restructuring in order to put the peak at the end. Especially if the translation is being done into poetry, such reordering of verses should be encouraged in any language where chiastic structures are not appreciated. If the version is for a normal Bible rather than a special poetic portion, it may be advisable to put both the original verse numbers in parentheses and the combined numbers with a hyphen to help readers find specific verses.

The author is convinced that marking peaks in some equivalent receptor language form will be a major help for the reader to see the main intent of the original. The peak of the poem will become clear to the modern reader as it was to the Hebrew audience, who could hear in the recitation whether the lines varied in length and the poem was chiastic, or if the lines were all the same length leading to a final peak. Although a listening audience will not be helped by seeing printing changes, the oral reader can immediately note which line is the peak and can add articulatory emphasis. This will bring the translation closer to a functional equivalence for a very difficult but important stylistic feature.

References

Alter, Robert. 1985. *The Art of Biblical Poetry*. New York: Basic Books.

Andersen, Francis I, and A. Dean Forbes. 1989. *The Vocabulary of the Old Testament*. Rome: Pontificio Istituto Biblico.

Andersen, Francis I, and David N. Freedman. 1980. *Hosea* (The Anchor Bible). Garden City, New York: Doubleday.

Bliese, Loren F. 1982. "Metrical Chiasmus, Peak and Structural Symmetry in Hosea." Paper presented at the 1982 UBS AFRETCON Workshop in Kenya, revised 1993.

———. 1983-7. UBS workshop papers on Isaiah 20, and Psalms 25, 33, 34, and 145, and a manuscript describing metrical chiasmus in Psalm 137 by both word-accents and syllables.

———. 1988a. "Metrical Sequences and Climax in the Poetry of Joel." *Occasional Papers in Translation and Textlinguistics* 2.4, 52-84.

———. 1988b. "Chiastic Structures, Peaks and Cohesion in Nehemiah 9.6-37." *The Bible Translator* 39.2, 208-215.

———. 1990. "Structurally Marked Peak in Psalms 1–24." *Occasional Papers in Translation and Textlinguistics* 4.4, 266-321.

———. 1991. "Translating Psalm 23 in Traditional Afar Poetry." Paper presented at the 1991 UBS Triennial Translation Workshop.

———. 1992. "Structural Prominence in Second Isaiah 40, 45 and Servant Poems." Paper presented at the 1992 UBS Translation Workshop in Nairobi.

———. 1993a. "A Cryptic Chiastic Acrostic: Finding Meaning from Structure in the Poetry of Nahum." Paper presented at the Summer Institute of Linguistics Seminar on the Discourse Structure of Biblical Hebrew, Dallas, 1993.

———. 1993b. "Chiastic and Homogeneous Metrical Structures Enhanced by Word Patterns in Obadiah." *Journal of Translation and Textlinguistics* 6.3, 210-227.

———. 1993c. "The Poetics of Habakkuk." Paper presented at the 1993 UBS Translation Workshop in Nairobi.

Cotterell, Peter, and Max Turner. 1989. *Linguistics and Biblical Interpretation.* London: SPCK.

Kugel, James. 1981. *The Idea of Biblical Poetry: Parallelism and Its History.* New York: Yale University Press.

Longacre, Robert. 1983. *The Grammar of Discourse.* New York: Plenum.

Shoshany, Ronit. 1986. "Prosodic Structures in Jeremiah's Poetry." *Folia Linguistica Historica* 7.1, 167-206.

Watson, Wilfred G.E. 1987. *Classical Hebrew Poetry.* Sheffield: Journal for the Study of the Old Testament, Supplement 26.

Yee, Gale A. 1987. *Composition and Tradition in the Book of Hosea: A Redaction Critical Investigation.* SBL Dissertation Series 102. Atlanta: Scholars Press.

Youngblood, Ronald. 1989. "Divine Names in the Book of Psalms: Literary Structures and Number Patterns." *JANES* 19, 171-181.

Hebrew Poetry and the Text of the Song of Songs

Robert A. Bascom

Introduction

This paper will deal with Hebrew poetry and textual criticism of the Hebrew Bible. More specifically, it will look at the examples from the *Preliminary and Interim Report on the Hebrew Old Testament Text Project* (HOTTP) with regard to the Song of Songs/Solomon and examine the results in light of Hebrew poetic principles. Textual criticism has its own rules and cannot be bound to any ideas of poetics in order to determine the best attested text. But often support from poetics can be had, once a text-critical decision is taken, and even the process of trying to understand what earlier hearers and readers understood a particularly difficult text to be saying is often aided by our understanding of Hebrew poetry. Since Hebrew poetry is largely defined by parallel lines, this feature is naturally the most prominent in this study. There is much more to Hebrew poetics, however, and such things as terseness, elaboration, imagery, inclusio, and even chiasmus need to be taken into account at times in order to make sense of the text. Since HOTTP will be used throughout, it will not be often cited explicitly but can be taken to be the direct or indirect source of the suggestions presented unless stated otherwise. Not all examples will be treated, since not all will have demonstrable poetic significance (e.g., 4.12, where the options "fountain/garden" are equally arguable poetically), some are text-critical differences which are later neutralized in translation (e.g., 1.7, where "veiled/vagabond," which though different enough on the surface, in the end refer to the same thing—a prostitute), and some are simply too complex for such an overview (e.g., 7.9, and verse 2, which contains several interrelated problems in one verse). It should be noted that, though for reasons of brevity and simplicity HOTTP will define the parameters of the text-critical discussion in this section, there are other text-critical issues it does not cover, as well as some further dimensions to a few of the problems it does discuss. It remains to be seen to what degree an understanding of Hebrew poetry and its implementation in analysis could help shed light on these cases.[1]

Examples from the Song of Songs / Solomon

1.4	MT	**"rightly do they love you"**
	Conjecture	"more than songs your caresses"

Context: 1.2-4

O that you would kiss me with the kisses of your mouth!
For your love is better than wine,
    your anointing oils are fragrant,
your name is oil poured out;
    therefore **the maidens love you**.
Draw me after you, let us make haste.
    The king has brought me into his chambers.
We will exult and rejoice in you;
    we will extol your love more than wine;
    rightly do **they love you**.

This first case is interesting in that understanding MT as well as the conjecture both involve an understanding of Hebrew poetics. The conjecture is (understandably) more straightforward. If "extol your love more than wine" is to have a further parallel than already exists in the previous "We will exult and rejoice in you," then "more than songs your caresses" makes a nice chiastic parallel line, reusing the verb "extol" from the first line to complete the meaning. Not just vowels must be changed in the MT text, however, but a *waw* must become a *yod* and another *yod* must change position in order to achieve this parallel structure. On the other hand, if MT as we have it is taken as it is, the parallel line can still be seen, but at more of a distance. The end of verse three is "therefore the maidens love you," which would be nicely paralleled and intensified by "rightly do they [the maidens] love you." This is supported by the parallel comparison of love and wine just prior to this proposed parallel, itself intensified by "extol." Here as elsewhere poetry does not determine text criticism, but if the text is a poetic one, we would expect text-critical analysis to reveal a poetical text of some kind (though perhaps not the most obvious kind).

1.5 MT **"of Solomon"**
Conjecture "of Shalma"

Context: 1.5
I am very **dark** but **comely**,
O daughters of Jerusalem,
like the **tents of Kedar**,
like the **curtains of Solomon**.

Here the question is whether sense can be made of using "of Solomon" to modify "curtains" rather than conjecturing "of Shalma" (presumed to be a place name by Jerusalem Bible (JB) and New English Bible [NEB]). A nonliteral adjectival force ("Solomonic") befitting a poetic text can be understood for the phrase in question. This would turn it into a synonym for "majestic, regal" rather than let it stand as a literal statement about the ownership of the curtains or repointing to read "Shalma." This reading, while disregarding a more direct parallel structure (where Shalma and Kedar are both places/people of dark tents), has the advantage of uncovering a more complex parallel structure: "dark . . . like the tents of Kedar . . . comely . . . like the curtains of Solomon." This would play off the rustic dark tents of Kedar against the royal purple/crimson curtains of Solomon.

2.5 MT **"sustain me" (plural imperative)**
Conjecture "he sustained me"

Context: 2.4-5
He brought me to the banqueting house,
and his banner over me was love.
Sustain me with raisins,
refresh me with apples;
for I am sick with love.

The easier reading would be the conjectured agreement with the verb tense of the preceding verse ("he brought me in . . ."). But poetically, as well as text-critically, one could defend MT. An aside to the chorus parallel to what we have in 2.7, 3.5, and elsewhere would be a slightly unusual but perfectly poetical way to understand this text. The close parallel ("refresh me") in the verse supports this reading further. In fact it actually makes a certain kind of sense addressed to the chorus, since it is a proposed solution to a problem (love-sickness) brought about by the man, and thus appealing to him directly for help is less likely than to others at this point. One is reminded of famous fainting scenes in literature and the arts ("Catch me, I think I'm going to faint!"—addressed to no one in particular). That the plural imperative is also masculine is no more a problem here than in 2.7, 3.5 and many other places in the Hebrew Bible. In fact the feminine plural in general is reserved for cases where no man could possibly be included.

2.7; 3.5; 8.4	MT	**"love"**
	Vulgate (V)	
	Translational adjustment	"the loved (woman)"

Context: 2.7; 3.5; 8.4

I adjure you, O daughters of Jerusalem,
by the gazelles or the hinds of the field,
that you stir not up nor awaken **love** until it please.

Depending on one's interpretation, this case could well be neutralized in many translations. That is to say, if "love" is taken as a poetical way of referring to the beloved, it comes out the same as the translational adjustment "the loved (woman)/beloved." It is important to note, however, that the use of "love" in this way, or its use in a more general or ambiguous manner, would be something we would expect of poetry. This would be terse but rich imagery, since either of the parties, both, or their passion, or all of the above could be referenced with this one word.

3.1,2	MT	**"and I did not find him"**
	LXX	"and I did not find him, I called him, but he did not answer me"

Context: 3.1,2; 5.6

Upon my bed by night
    I sought him whom my soul loves;
I sought him, **but found him not**;
    [I called him, but he gave no answer]
I will rise and go about the city,
    in the streets and in the squares;
I will seek him whom my soul loves.
    I sought him, **but found him not**
    [I called him, but he gave no answer].

Poetically the argument could go either way, since terseness favors MT and elaborative parallelism favors LXX. Text-critically, however, there can be no doubt that LXX is assimilating to 5.6.[2]

3.10	MT	**"with love by the daughters of Jerusalem"**
	Conjecture	"with ebony. Daughters of Jerusalem . . ."

Context: 3.9-11

King Solomon made himself a palanquin
    from the wood of Lebanon.
He made its posts of silver,
    its back of gold, its seat of purple;
it was lovingly wrought within
    by the **daughters of Jerusalem**.
Go forth, O **daughters of Zion**,
    and behold King Solomon,
with the crown with which his mother crowned him
    on the day of his wedding,
    on the day of the gladness of his heart.

Here NJB has taken "daughters of Jerusalem" as belonging to the next verse, substituting it for that verse's "daughters of Zion" (not found in LXX) and correcting "love" to "ebony." NEB keeps the repetition but puts it all in the next verse and translates the remaining word of 3.10 as "leather." The argument text-critically (made by NJB in its notes) is that this kind of repetition of daughters of Jerusalem/Zion may represent a gloss which eventually got into the text.[3] Poetic repetition is also possible, however, and the fact that the parallels occur in different verses and in different levels of the discourse makes the juxtaposition all the more striking. Grammatically the first case is backgrounded, part of a prepositional phrase modifying a part of an object foregrounded in the preceding section (Solomon's carriage). The second is foregrounded, the subject of imperative verbs, while the parallel to the carriage ("with the *crown*") is backgrounded in another prepositional phrase. That the first phrase's key term is the more straightforward "Jerusalem" and the second is the less common, more poetic "Zion" is further evidence that poetic conventions are being followed. More to the point, however, is that the repetition of these "daughters" may well have been used to tie the different sections of text together, thus serving a discourse as well as a poetic function.[4]

4.1 MT **"from mount Gilead"**
6.5 MT "from Gilead"

Context: 4.1b; 6.5b

Your hair is like a flock of goats,
moving down from **(Mount) Gilead**.

In this case, Revised Standard Version (RSV) has assimilated 4.1 to 6.5[5], and NEB has assimilated 6.5 to 4.1. These cases have to do with poetry in that we are reminded that variation, however minor, is as important a part of poetry as is repetition of various kinds. Assimilation is therefore not only unsound text-critically but should be resisted on poetic grounds as well. Of course, this case would often be neutralized in translation, but even there it serves as a reminder that stylistic variation is very much a part of the original text and should be considered in translation.

4.5 MT **"that feed among the lilies"**
Conjecture []

Context: 4.5

Your two breasts are like two **fawns**,
twins of a gazelle,
that feed among the **lilies**.

NEB seemingly does not tolerate the poetic elaboration at this point (or considers it a gloss based on 2.16) and so misses one of the most beautiful descriptions of the human (female) form in the Hebrew Bible (Revised English Bible [REB] restores it, however). Many commentators see the brown fawns/white lilies color contrast here as referring to the darker color of the nipples of the breasts against the lighter background of the torso. Even in 2.16 ("he pastures his flock among the lilies) NEB seems to have missed a good deal of the imagery, as it drops "pastures his flocks" in favor of "delights in." If "flocks" are a reference to the dark hair of the man, and the lilies again are the breasts of the woman (cf. 4.1, 6.3,5), we have a vivid image of her cradling his head in her bosom.

4.10	MT	**"love"**
	LXX, V (Misunderstanding of linguistic data}	"breasts"

Context: 4.10

How sweet is your **love**, my sister, my bride!
how much better is your love than wine,
and the fragrance of your oils than any spice!

Again NEB has chosen not to follow MT, and here MT has as good a foundation if attention is given to Hebrew poetic structure.[6] The intensification in the verse's second line "your love is even better than wine" usually would require an equally or more general parallel. Something as specific a "breasts," while not impossible, would violate the normal rules of general-to-specific (and not the other way around) in Hebrew poetry.[7]

4.13	MT	**"shoots"**
	Conjecture	"your two cheeks"

Context: 4.12-13

A garden locked is my sister, my bride,
a garden locked, a fountain sealed.
Your **shoots** are an orchard of pomegranates
with all choicest fruits,
henna with nard.

A literal term in the middle of an imagistic section is not impossible but would have the effect of making "cheeks" the basis of comparison for all the figures which follow, which seems to be rather overdoing it. The broader, all-inclusive image "shoots," on the other hand, leaves open more possibilities, both physical and emotional, and also fits in nicely with the imagery of the garden in verse twelve.

4.13	MT	**"henna with nard"**
	Conjecture	[]

Context: 4.13-14

Your shoots are an orchard of pomegranates
with all choicest fruits,
henna with **nard**,
nard and saffron, calamus and cinnamon,
with all trees of frankincense,
myrrh and aloes,
with all chief spices—

The mention of nard (a fragrant spice) at the end of this verse nicely weaves together with its mention in the next line. That repetition is doubtless the reason for NEB's dropping it (but cf. REB, which puts it back!). The forms of the word are dissimilar (singular/plural), however, so scribal sight/sound errors are unlikely. As to repetition as such, 4.8's "Come with me from Lebanon . . ." gives us a good example of repetition/variation possibilities in this kind of poetry.

4.15	MT	**"gardens"**
	Conjecture	"my garden"

Context: 4.12–5.1a

A **garden** locked is my sister, my bride,
a **garden** locked, a **fountain** sealed.
Your shoots are an orchard of pomegranates
with all the choicest fruits,
henna with nard,
nard and saffron, calamus and cinnamon,
with all the trees of frankincense,

myrrh with aloes,
    with all chief spices—
a garden **fountain**, a well of living water,
    and flowing streams from Lebanon.

Awake, O north wind,
    and come, O south wind!
Blow upon my garden,
    let its fragrance be wafted abroad.
Let my beloved come to his **garden**,
    and eat of its choicest fruits.

I have entered my **garden** . . .

NEB here has given verses 15 and 16 to the woman ("Bride"), leaving the mention of a fountain in verse 12 without the elaboration it receives in verses 15 and 16 if they are on the lips of the man, as is the case in other versions. Understanding "gardens" adjectivally modifying "fountain" in verse 15, however, allows for a neat two-part poetic structure to the section in 12-15. First verse 12 mentions both garden and fountain, in that order. Then verses 13-14 describe the garden, and verse 15 describes the fountain. Finally, verses 4.16–5.1 close with "garden" once again, forming a chiastic structure of the key words "garden-fountain-fountain-garden" and providing a neatly structured closing to this section of poetic discourse.[8]

5.6	MT	**"when he spoke"**
	Conjecture	"when he escaped"

Context: 5.4-6

My beloved put his hand to the latch,
    and my heart was thrilled within me.
I arose to open to my beloved,
    and my hands dripped with myrrh,
I opened to my beloved,
    but my beloved had turned and gone.
My soul failed me when he spoke.
I sought him, but found him not;
    I called him, but he gave no answer.

The case here is simply repointing (changing the vowels) of MT, and an easier, more logical reading would result. If MT is taken to be the reading, however, the line in 6 would be a distant chiastic parallel to verse four:

4	6b
When my love put his hand to the latch,	My soul failed me
my heart was thrilled within me	when he spoke

Once again this chiasmus could be a significant discourse feature (cf. previous example and 3.10), marking off the subsection of verses 4-6 within the larger unit of 2-8. Of the modern versions, GNB alone has noted this structure and reproduced it in its format.[9]

5.11	MT	**"black as a raven"**
	Conjecture	[]

Context: 5.11-15

His head is the finest **gold**;
his locks are wavy,
black as a raven.
His eyes are like doves
beside springs of water,
bathed in milk,
fitly set.
His cheeks are like beds of spices,
yielding fragrance.
His lips are lilies,
distilling myrrh.
His arms are rounded **gold**,
set with jewels.
His body is ivory work,
encrusted with sapphires.
His legs are alabaster columns,
set upon bases of **gold**.

Here the dropping of the last line of this verse would make it fit better into the general pattern of the section (verses 10-16), which has a series of couplets (and one double couplet—verse 12) describing with metaphors and similes the physical beauty of the man from head to toe. Not only that, "black as a raven" seems to contrast with, if not entirely contradict, "gold" (=blond or red?) in the first line. This should not be pushed too far, however, in light of the following: 1) In 11-15 "gold" is used three times, of head (11), arms (14), and feet 15). 2) Of head and feet the term "gold" is not the usual *zahav* (as in 14) but *paz* "refined gold." Thus this merism/inclusio using *paz* makes the man generally "golden" from head to foot and should not be taken to refer as directly to the hair as the line "black as a raven" would. That takes care of the supposed contradiction and leaves only the problem of the break in the two-line couplet sequence, certainly not a valid text-critical argument in any case, and poetically justifiable in terms of the principle of unexpected variation/elaboration as a counterpoint to repetition and orderly structure.[10] What is more, the next verse (12) itself breaks the semantic structure with a double couplet describing the beloved's eyes.

5.13 MT "towers of"
LXX **"producing"**

Context: 5.11-15

His head is the finest gold;
his locks are wavy,
black as a raven.
His eyes are like doves
beside springs of water,
bathed in milk,
fitly set.
His cheeks are like beds of spices,
yielding fragrance.
His lips are lilies,
distilling myrrh.
His arms are rounded gold,
set with jewels.
His body is ivory work,
encrusted with sapphires.
His legs are alabaster columns,
set upon bases of gold.

Text-critically HOTTP could not decide, and poetically two opposing arguments are also possible. The first, supporting MT, would see "towers of perfumes" as intensification of the first line's "beds of spices." The second, supporting the repointing of the Hebrew represented by LXX, would show the couplets in 11-15 as all moving logically forward in the second line, not repeating or even intensifying. For example, in verse 13b "His lips are lilies, distilling (producing) liquid myrrh" would give a more orderly poetic parallel to 13a's "yielding fragrance." This argument in favor of LXX seems better contextually. Here is a rare case where the consideration of context could take poetics beyond a supporting role and perhaps even help break a text-critical impasse.

6.4	MT	**"terrible as an army with banners"**
	Conjecture	[]

Context: 6.4-5a,10

You are beautiful as Tirzah, my love,
comely as Jerusalem,
terrible as an army with banners.
Turn away your eyes from me,
for they disturb me—
. . .
Who is this that looks forth like the dawn,
fair as the moon, bright as the sun,
terrible as an army with banners?

The section 4-10 begins (almost) and ends with this phrase. It should be understood as an inclusio, therefore, and translated with MT in both places. NEB, which drops it in verse 4 (REB again corrects this, cf. other cases of this above), translates the same Hebrew phrase in verse 10 as "majestic as the starry heavens," which would probably be closer to the force of this powerful image in that context ("dawn . . . moon . . . sun"). On the other hand, the army with its flags waving fits better with the mention of cities (or city-states) in verse 4. It would be better to preserve the repetition in translation if possible, but to try also to preserve the play on the sparkling heavenly hosts with an army on the move with its banners flying. Both images are striking and should not be ignored. This could probably only be accomplished in a note, but NIV makes a brave attempt by repeating "majestic" and the rest according to context. GNB, on the other hand, has translated contextually only, with an identical note in each case stating "Hebrew unclear" (a case of inadvertently representing the inclusio by means of a note!).

7.6[7.7]	MT	"in delights"
	Aquila (α')	**"daughter of delights"**

Context: 7.6

How fair and pleasant you are,
    O loved one, **delectable maiden**!

Text-critically, haplography apparently is the cause for "daughter of" dropping out of the MT text, as can be seen in the Hebrew orthography (*bat t. . .> bat . . .*). Poetically this is supported by the fact that "daughter of delights" (RSV "delectable maiden") stands much better in apposition with "O loved one" than does "in delights." It is possible to read the verse without (or with distant) apposition with "fair and pleasant" as "How fair and pleasant you are, O loved one, how delightful," but this would be unusual grammar, even for Hebrew poetry.

8.2	MT	**"you/she would teach me"**
	LXX (MT 3.4)	"and into my mother's dwelling"

Context: 8.2; 3.4b

I would lead you and bring you
    into the house of my mother,
    [into the chamber of her that conceived me]
    /**and she would teach me**
. . .
I held him, and would not let him go
    until I brought him into the house of my mother,
    into the chamber of her that conceived me.

Text-critically the Septuagint assimilates to 3.4, but what makes it relevant for a discussion of poetry is that it can be argued that in doing so, the Septuagint fills out the parallel structure which obviously has been truncated in the process of textual transmission. Thus the twin verbs at the beginning would each have a prepositional phrase complement:

"lead . . . into the house of my mother" and "bring . . . into the chamber of the one who conceived me." There is a problem with this analysis, however, starting with the allegedly parallel case in 3.4. There one verb ("brought") takes the two prepositional phrases under consideration as dual complements. Thus one could as easily expect two verbs to share the same complement, which is in fact not uncommon in Hebrew poetry (cf. 2.7/3.5/8.4, where "love/beloved" is the complement of the two negative imperatives "do not stir up/do not awaken"). This would leave the line open for the addition of the surprising element "(and) you/she would teach me." Surprising, but wholly in accord with the rules of intensification/specification, here apparently developed in a narrative mode. Thus a potential two-line verse is converted into a three-line verse, with minor specification ("lead/bring") in the second "line" (really just a verb and its recycled complement) and narrative specification/intensification in the third line.

Conclusion

As we have seen, Hebrew poetic structures do not usually play a determinative role in textual criticism. On the other hand they help us to understand the possible meaning of the text, especially when that text is under suspicion of being textually corrupt. That is not to say that poetics should be used only to justify conservative textual decisions or rescue hopelessly obscure texts. Arguments must be weighed on both sides and considered as part of the larger picture of interpretation as a whole. Poetic understanding can help us interpret the text given to us by text-criticism, however, and even play a supporting role in making text-critical judgments. Rarely it can even tip the scale in close text-critical decisions. After all, if it is poetry, it should sound like it.

HOTTP (Preliminary and Interim Report), used as a guide in this investigation, takes no explicit account of poetics in its text-critical decisions, but the team members were all Hebrew scholars who knew Hebrew poetry as well as Hebrew grammar, and at times we may have been walking in their footsteps unawares. Neither the Preliminary and Interim or Final Reports of HOTTP have been as useful to translators as was hoped at the outset. A major reason has been the lack of explicit information about how text-critical decisions were reached on the one hand (Preliminary and Interim Report), and an overwhelming amount of technical detail difficult to weigh and understand by anyone other than a expert in the field on the other (Final Report). Perhaps more explicit attention to features such as poetics—certainly a part of the process in text-critical decisions—would make the valuable work done by the committee more accessible to the interested nonspecialist, and to translators in particular.

Finally, if some of the above scattered observations about discourse structure (3.10, 4.13, 4.15, similarly 1.4, 5.6) in the Song of Songs can be brought together into a coherent statement about the style of the author(s), it is that they "weave" with images and words, with repetition serving to unite across grammatical and poetic boundaries. This perhaps gives us more confidence in confirming our text-critical judgments, but we cannot allow it to guide us in text-critical decisions (cf. 7.6). To do that would be to fall back into the trap of using preconceived ideas about what the text *should* say in order to determine what the text *does* say.

Notes

1. RSV will be used as a basis for scripture quotation throughout, but the author has taken translational liberties in order to make certain points. The HOTTP translation has also been used at times in the text-critical examples.

2. Interestingly, RSV follows LXX in verse 1 with a note, but MT in verse 2 without a note.

3. This is a simplified explanation of JB/NJB's adaptation of the textual apparatus in BHS.

4. I owe this particular discourse insight to Ernst Wendland, who graciously read the paper and improved it greatly by his comments.

5. It is possible also that RSV has actually assimilated 6.5 to 4.1 along with NEB, if RSV's "slopes" represents implicitly "Mount" in its translation.

6. Actually NEB does not follow LXX and Vulgate either, which translate "breasts" in both cases. It is only a matter of pointing, and though the harder reading text-critically would be "breasts," the HOTTP committee apparently thought the rare poetic form of "love" has been mistaken for

the common word for "breasts" by the ancient translators.

7. D.J.A. Clines ("The Parallelism of Greater Precision") tries to bring a greater degree of precision to Kugel's "A, and what's more B" paradigm of parallelism. Clines points out that the relationship is most often one of *specification,* so that the formula in the majority of cases should be "A, *namely* B." He admits at the same time that the possibilities for the relationship between the two lines are so varied that the general formula should perhaps be even more general than Kugel's—"A is related to B."

8. Once again I owe the discourse insight to Ernst Wendland.

9. On the other hand, GNB unnecessarily restructures the line into "How I wanted to hear his voice." The use of a past tense is correct, but it should be understood as "My soul *had* failed me."

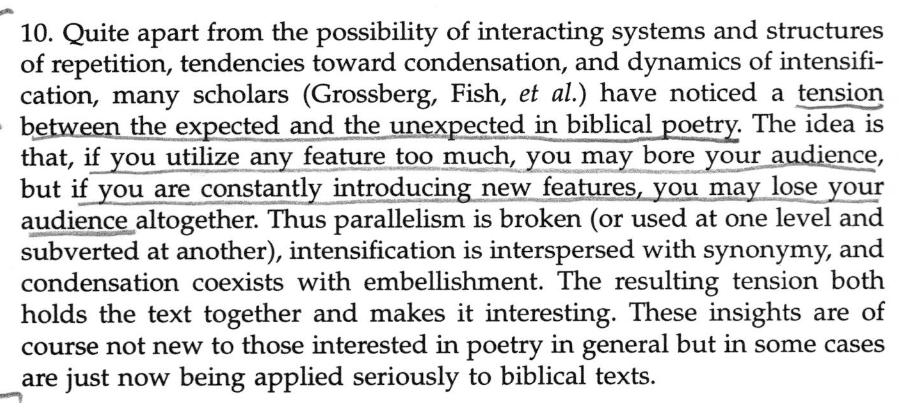

10. Quite apart from the possibility of interacting systems and structures of repetition, tendencies toward condensation, and dynamics of intensification, many scholars (Grossberg, Fish, *et al.*) have noticed a tension between the expected and the unexpected in biblical poetry. The idea is that, if you utilize any feature too much, you may bore your audience, but if you are constantly introducing new features, you may lose your audience altogether. Thus parallelism is broken (or used at one level and subverted at another), intensification is interspersed with synonymy, and condensation coexists with embellishment. The resulting tension both holds the text together and makes it interesting. These insights are of course not new to those interested in poetry in general but in some cases are just now being applied seriously to biblical texts.

Poetry, Prose, and Their Relationship: Some Reflections Based on Judges 4 and 5

Graham S. Ogden

Not very often do we have the opportunity to compare two formally different literary accounts of one event. However, in the Deborah story of Judges 4 and 5 we are in the fortunate position of having access to two distinctive accounts of her exploits. Chapter 4 presents the story in narrative form, while chapter 5 is in the poetic mode. A comparison of these two accounts may assist us in our attempt to define more closely the relationship between these two forms, as well as some special features of Hebrew poetry.

The present study will deliberately focus upon those points at which the two chapters or accounts differ. This approach should not be interpreted, however, as implying that these chapters have little in common with each other. Indeed, the common ground they share is perhaps more important theologically than any of their literary and other differences. It is important to affirm that both accounts acknowledge that it is Yahweh who ultimately gives Israel the victory over the enemy. Whether that victory is achieved through human agency or through divine intervention, the emphasis is still the same, namely that Yahweh is the one who is mightily at work to bring his people out of bondage.

However, despite their common elements, it is nevertheless the differences in the accounts which is our primary concern here, for it is in this focus that we believe the poetic and prose forms can be more readily identified and catalogued.

This study will not engage in a discussion about the present canonical shape of the text in which the poetic version follows the narrative account. There are those who believe that the poetic account is placed after the narrative account so that the reader of the poem will be able to supplement from the narrative information lacking in the poem, that the poetic version presupposes knowledge of the former. This may be the editorial principle at work, but it has little to do with the characteristic features of prose and poetic *forms* in which the two accounts were created. The question is even more complex when we recognize that chapter 5 represents one of the oldest literary pieces in the Hebrew Bible, dating, according to Freedman (1975, page 3), to the twelfth century B.C.

1. Distinctive Features of Judges 4 and 5

A. We begin with a surface-level examination of the differences between the two accounts of the Deborah incident. These differences are well-known and have been frequently documented. All the standard commentaries make note of them. We list them here for convenience:

a) The narrative account in 4.4-22 is framed by the "deuteronomic" material into which it is inserted, while in chapter 5 we have an account that gives details of the event within a liturgical framework.

b) The narrative account conforms to the "Holy War" concept, in which Yahweh leads Israel into battle and gives them the victory as the enemy troops panic before the Israelites, while in chapter 5 Yahweh, whose appearance is accompanied by cosmic upheaval, uses those cosmic powers and natural phenomena to defeat the enemy.

c) Jabin king of Hazor, represented by his general Sisera, is the antagonist in chapter 4; but Jabin is not mentioned in chapter 5, giving the impression that it is Sisera and his army alone who confront Israel.

d) Zebulun and Naphtali are identified as the tribes joining the conflict in chapter 4; chapter 5 lists many more tribes as having been involved in some manner, though that list climaxes with mention of Zebulun and Naphtali.

e) Barak's role in chapter 5 is almost without mention, in contrast to chapter 4.

f) Chapter 4 places the battle near Mt. Tabor, whereas chapter 5 has it further south, on the opposite side of the Kishon, near Megiddo.

g) Sisera is killed while asleep according to chapter 4, but he seems to be standing and still drinking when he is struck in chapter 5.

h) Chapter 4 does not make mention of Meroz, an otherwise unknown location whose people are the subject of the curse in chapter 5.

i) Chapter 5 adds a scene involving Sisera's mother and friends awaiting his return. Such a scene is not to be found in chapter 4.

These are the more obvious differences in the content of the two accounts. However, these surface-level content variations, while of considerable significance, cannot explain the full extent of the differences between the two forms of the presentation. Of greater importance are the distinctive literary and discourse features of each presentation. Only by focusing here can we begin to come to a fuller appreciation of the nature of poetic presentation and its fundamental difference from prose.

B. Here we turn to a closer examination of the variations between the two accounts, looking particularly at their rhetorical and discourse features:

a) The introduction provided in 4.1-3 points to Israel's relapse into evil, resulting in Yahweh bringing them under the control of the Canaanite king Jabin of Hazor. Sisera, his general, is also identified in terms of his role and birthplace. Israel's response to oppressive treatment is mentioned, along with the military might of the Canaanites. None of this information is presented in chapter 5, which launches directly into a call to praise Yahweh, before whom heaven and earth, the whole cosmos, tremble.

There is an inclusio which holds 5.2-9 together in the call to "bless the Lord," indicating the liturgical setting in which the song had its origin and through which it was preserved. This call to the hearers invites their response, indicating the essentially oral nature of this work. We can imagine the people responding in praise and blessing for what Yahweh has done.

The poetic version then makes no attempt to identify the main actors in this drama, nor to give a reason, theological or other, for the situation in which the Israelites found themselves. We might conclude from this that the poem is not really interested in providing these "historical" facts, or to put the poem in some kind of historical or social setting. Although there is some mention of people and places in the poem, their appearance borders on the incidental, providing nothing more than the most basic information as to who actually fought whom. Even if we were to agree with those who suggest that chapter 5 presupposes familiarity with the details of chapter 4, the song nevertheless conforms to the poetic mode's sparseness of detail. We can see in this the poet's differing concern and approach; such details are not essential to the poem's purpose as a hymn of praise for what Yahweh did for Israel. The absence of so much background information is also consistent with the use of very generalized language in the Psalms, or in Hebrew poetry in general.

b) In 5.6-9 there does seem to be some allusion to a historical situation giving rise to the song. We do not need to go into details about this at this point, except to note that there is some difference of opinion as to what that situation is, owing to the lack of certainty about the meaning of the verb *chadal* used in verse 7. Whatever the final answer to this problem might be, we note that the probable cause for the conflict is expressed in an indirect way. The phrase about new gods being chosen does not identify who it was that chose to worship them. We presume that it refers to Israel abandoning Yahweh, who revealed himself at Sinai and led the people through Edom and into the land of Canaan. We might also assume that the statement in verse 8 means that, because of this religious change of direction, Israel was to be punished. However, the listener is left to make this connection, to discover what the issue was that might have led to the battle. Such lack of precision is not surprising in poetic literature.

c) 4.4-10 describe the scene of the battle. Zebulun and Naphtali gather their troops and at the Kishon face the arrayed ranks of Sisera's army. Deborah's role is to enthuse the troops. Barak is invited to lead the attack. He holds a dialogue with Deborah about who should go, and his reluctance to go alone evokes Deborah's response that a woman will be the victorious one. None of this dialogue, whether imagined or real, is to be found in the poem. Indeed, one of the features of the poem is the absence of dialogue. This pattern is not dissimilar to other examples of poetic discourse where direct speech, if present, would be embedded.

d) 5.10-11 are addressed to the wealthy citizens of Israel. They are urged to tell of the Lord's triumphs, even though at this point in the poem or song there has been no mention of the battle or of victory. Nothing in chapter 4 reflects this appeal to citizens to acknowledge and affirm what Yahweh has done. This, however, is hardly surprising, as the poem is a call to people to praise Yahweh for what he has done. This feature of the poem is consistent with its function as a liturgical creation.

e) 4.11 is an anticipatory verse which introduces the reader to Heber the Kenite. What role he and his clan have is not to be made clear until much later. In the poem there is a reference to Heber the Kenite, but only as the husband of Jael (5.24). The information about his relationship with Sisera is not found there. As in (a) above, we note again an absence of purely informational elements. Yet we have here an important discourse feature in its use of an anticipatory element that causes the reader to expect to be told of the fuller significance of the comment at some later stage. Such a device draws the reader into the story.

f) 5.12-18 refers to Deborah and Barak. Deborah is to "lead on" with singing, while Barak is to "lead away" captives. This probably refers to Barak's subsequent victory over the enemy, presented here as a challenge to Barak or as an assurance of his subsequent victory.

There follows a review of the tribal responses to the call to join in the battle. The itemized list, a feature of poetic instruction throughout the Ancient Near East, indicates that some tribes were willing to join the fight, while others were not. Apart from Zebulun and Naphtali, other groups appear to have participated, according to chapter 5. The list given in chapter 4 limits participation in the battle to those two, and in 5.18 their mention at the close of the tribal list serves as the transition to the account of the battle itself.

The tribal list in chapter 5 contains numerous allusions about the tribes and the reasons why they did or did not heed the call to arms. These allusions clearly presuppose information about the tribes which presumably was known to the reader/hearer; there is nothing in the poem itself which can help clarify their meaning. These allusions offer another example of the nature of poetic presentation, namely that it is indirect and suggestive rather than explicit and informational.

g) The battle recounted in 4.12-16 gives considerable information about the Canaanite troops and their weapons, about Deborah's encouragement to Barak, and Yahweh's assistance to Israel by throwing the enemy into turmoil. Nothing in the poetic version can compare with this detail.

Chapter 5 presents the battle in quite different terms. Several Canaanite kings, none identified by name, oppose Israel. We are left to infer that, as hinted in verse 4, Yahweh caused a downpour which turned the Canaanite advantage in having cavalry into a liability, enabling Israel to win the victory.

h) In a dramatic image 5.22 anticipates the rain of death-dealing blows on Sisera's head in the description of his horse pounding its way from the scene of battle. Sisera attempts to escape. The same verb is used both of the horses' hoofs and Jael's hammering. The image also serves as a poetic adornment, onomatopoeic as well as extremely graphic. It is also anticipatory.

i) The anticipatory reference to Heber the Kenite in 4.11 is followed up in 4.17-18. It allows the explanation that Sisera sought out the Kenite because of preexisting friendly relations. By offering hospitality and then dispatching Sisera, Jael used deceit to defeat the enemy. This theme is to be found in other narratives of the Judges but not in the poem. The narrative form offers much more information about how Jael came to be in a position to save Israel by killing Sisera. This is consistent with the greater informational purpose of the story form.

j) Chapter 5 speaks only indirectly about the coming together of Jael and Sisera. The poet appears to want to go immediately to the heart of the matter, namely that Jael killed the enemy with a blow to the head. We have already seen how the versions of Sisera's death differ in detail, their only common point being the phrase "Jael the wife of Heber the Kenite" and the mention of the tent-peg weapon. Alternative words are used for the hammer.

k) Whereas chapter 4 relates Barak coming in search of Sisera only to find he has been killed by a woman, nothing of such consequence is mentioned in chapter 5, with its much more terse account. The poetic version limits details presumably to make for a more vivid account.

However, this points to another feature of poetic discourse, namely its terseness. On occasion, this is achieved by *parataxis*, the placing alongside one another of phrases, words, or situations which lack any connecting words or particles. For example, 5.8a makes an observation, while verse 8b follows with a rhetorical question whose relationship to the first half of the verse is not at first obvious. Hauser (1987:25) suggests that *parataxis* is perhaps the most important "key to understanding the poetic style." Kugel (1981:88) has made the point that terseness has the intention of heightening the writer's style.

This seeming lack of connection throughout poetry makes for a somewhat disjointed or uneven speech flow. It also calls upon the reader/hearer to provide the information left out by the poet. Such information may be part of the shared information which speaker and hearer have; on the other hand, it could be a poetic device which challenges the reader/hearer to make the necessary connections from within his or her own imagination.

l) The final major portion of chapter 5 is its imaginary account of Sisera's mother and lady friends awaiting his return in joyous expectation of sharing the spoils of victory. The reader knows that their wait is futile, but the scene painted by the poet is a very moving one; at the same time it is one which ridicules the enemy. It is a passage that evidences a truly fertile imagination. As such it is a highly significant element, one which points to a fundamental distinction between a prosaic treatment in which facts and details play a more prominent role, over against a poetic treatment in which the artist's imagination is given greater and freer rein.

A survey of this nature allows us to appreciate just how far apart in content, form, and focus are the two accounts. It is easier to describe the few phrases which they share in common than to try to detail their substantial differences.

What needs to be recognized here, of course, is that these variations between the two forms are dependent not only upon the fact that we are dealing with different literary forms, but also with different settings in the oral milieu of the community of faith. The story form has entertainment as well as historical and cultural transmission as its primary goals, while in the case of chapter 5 the poet has created a piece primarily for liturgical use, though certainly with entertainment and instruction as secondary purposes. These variant foci will inevitably have an impact such that the content and emphasis of each differs.

2. *Other Literary Features of Judges 5*

Apart from the differences of fact and emphasis listed above, there are a number of more microcosmic literary distinctions between the accounts to note. These distinctions assume greater importance as we try to define more closely how poetry differs from prose, or how song differs from story. It will help to clarify what is meant by the phrase "heightened language," as poetry is often characterized.

a) Like many poetic pieces, Judges 5 is marked by the frequent occurrence of *hapax legomena*. Examples can be found in 5.7—*perazon*, "warriors," or "rural population"(?)—or in 5.10, 11—"carpets" and "musicians." Also in 5.26 there is the word for "hammer," *halmot*, which falls into this category. This reminds us that the poet frequently calls upon vocabulary items, the root of which may be familiar, but whose appearance in the particular form found is not known elsewhere. Creativity of this kind inevitably gives the interpreter and translator a difficult time, but the poet delights in creating neologisms for familiar objects as part of a demonstration of literary skill, as well as from a desire to express ideas in a novel way. Alternatively the poet demonstrates his or her mastery of the full range of lexical items available in the language by calling on words and forms rarely used in more prosaic speech.

b) There can be, at chosen times, a lack of specificity about the description in poetry, bordering on the vague and deliberately unclear. It calls upon the reader to supply information either from a background shared with the author or from his or her own imagination. An example in 5.8 might be the phrase "then war was in the gates." There is no clear indication whose gates they were, who the combatants were, nor what the direct cause of the war was. Similarly "Then down to the gates marched the people of the Lord" at the end of verse 11 is a clause whose connection with the preceding and following material is difficult to describe and define. At times this lack of specificity is due to allusive expressions such as "And Dan, why did he abide with the ships? Asher sat still at the coast of the sea . . ." (5.17). On other occasions such vagueness is due to ellipsis—we are called to supply for ourselves the information that there was a storm creating a flood between verses 20 and 21. The poet sees no necessity to give all the details, preferring to tease out the reader's imaginative powers. Kugel (1981:92), in commenting on this feature of poetry, also notes that "it is left to the reader or listener to figure it out . . . . The absence of normal signposts heightens attention and sets the discourse off as special and carefully made."

c) Repetition of key words, and especially verbs, is an important feature of this poem. For example, in the description of the death of Sisera in verse 27 we find "He *sank*, he *fell*, he *lay still* at her feet; at her feet he *sank*, he *fell*; where he *sank*, there he *fell* dead." This powerful description of Sisera's death recreates the scene in the hearer's mind. The repetition not only provides emphasis, it also slows down the pace of the story, so that at its climax we move into slow motion; the poet wants the reader actually to visualize the enemy gradually falling to the ground under the rain of blows from Jael's hammer.

Repetition of phrases and clauses has various purposes, one of which is to mark units which have a degree of unity. For example, the entire battle scene in 5.12-23 is identified by the phrase "against the mighty" in verses 13 and 23. The clause "Among the clans of Reuben there were great searchings of heart" has a probable structural function as it straddles the central line of the entire poem.

d) In combination with repetition we also find here several examples in which a series of synonymous verbs adds weight to the action. Generally this is done in sets of three: 5.4, "the earth trembled, and the heavens dropped, yea, the clouds dropped water" (RSV); 5.10, "you who ride on tawny asses, you who sit on rich carpets and you who walk by the way"; or 5.26, "she struck Sisera a blow, she crushed his head, she shattered and pierced his temple." In this pattern we note a feature already well known and documented in other early Israelite poems. For example, in Exodus 15 we have a nominal example in verse 2 with "my strength . . . my song . . . my salvation"; in verse 8 we note three synonymous verbs, "piled up . . . stood up . . . congealed." Additionally there is an example in verse 15, "dismayed . . . trembling . . . melted away," all describing the fearful reaction of Israel's enemies. Although this may prove to be a stylistic feature favored by a particular writer rather than being intrinsic to poetic form as such, it is a characteristic one which we should note.

e) Deborah's Song also provides evidence of another poetic device, namely what Alter (1985:23) calls "incremental repetition." This is the form in which a second line repeats the first, but in doing so adds an item which is generally implicit in the first line. Some examples in the Song are: 5.3, where we find ". . . to the Lord" followed by ". . . to the Lord, the God of Israel"; or in 5.23, "Curse Meroz, . . . curse oh curse its inhabitants," and ". . . to the aid of the Lord . . . to the aid of the Lord among his warriors."

f) In 5.22 we find a repetition of the verb "gallop," in which there is created the sound of Sisera's horses pounding their way from the battlefield. It is also anticipatory, for the same verb is used of the hammer blows which Jael rains down on Sisera's head. There is a superb link between the two actions provided by the poet. Thus repetition and the piling up of synonymous vocabulary items with onomatopoeic purpose allows the poet to create atmosphere, to evoke sounds and feelings, to draw the hearer/reader fully into the scene. This, together with the challenge to the reader to fill the gaps left in the account, is integral to the "suggestive" nature of poetry; it is evocative, it calls the reader to use his or her imagination to complete the picture. Additionally the succession of polysyllabic words evokes a sense of speed, suggesting an increased tempo in the action.

This feature is an excellent example of the orality of poetry. By this is meant the creative process, the poet's choice of words and entire presentation, which has in view the oral repetition of the work. It is not intended primarily as a work to be read and pondered at leisure, though that is not excluded. However, the primary focus at both the moment of creation and subsequent recital is that the poem should be heard, sung and recited. This fits with the opening call in verse 3, "Hear, . . . give ear . . ." We look for those markers and features that are peculiar to the oral form.

However, we cannot deny that in many cases, especially in Judges, the storytellers have also aimed to create, in narrative form, a description which suggests and evokes rather than simply recounts cold details. This arises because the stories, preserved in the text as it is now, existed and were handed down in oral form over an extended period. They were told to entertain as well as to instruct; to convey attitudes and values as well as to preserve the memory of the past. This is certainly true of the Ehud story, for example, in 3.12-30. It has all the elements of the "Irish/Polish joke" form in which one group of people tells of an incident involving themselves and another group in such a way as to ridicule the other party. What we can claim about the poetic form of Judges 5 over against chapter 4 is that its more poetic elements take these features to a new and much higher level.

g) Related to the previous point is the use of assonance, in which certain sound patterns are repeated, or similar sounds reiterated, for dramatic effect. The oral nature of poetry makes this feature an important one that translators should not overlook.

In 5.4, for example, we notice the heavy use of sibilant sounds—"*ts*," "*s*," "*sh*,"—together with the repetition of *mayim* in the final line, once as the ending of *shamayim* and once as the independent noun. In verse 6b there is the repetition of the "*kr/q*" and "*l*" sounds throughout.

h) Irony is an important element of the material in Judges. In the present story it is a significant component of both the narrative form and of the poem. That Sisera will be done to death by a woman represents a delightful turn of events, but it is even more poignant because the reader would automatically think of Deborah, the current leader, as the one to be so honored, whereas the truth is that it will be yet another woman, Jael. In the poem, no such expectation is created. However, the poem does preserve the overall irony of a woman dispatching Sisera with a household implement, not a weapon, when Sisera had at his disposal the full range of weapons such as the shields and spears mentioned in 5.8. We might also see irony in the imaginary scene of the women impatiently awaiting Sisera's victorious return. The reader knows that they wait in vain.

i) Chiasmus, of course, is a well-known feature of Hebrew poetry, though not exclusive to it. Its occurrence in poetry is more a matter of frequency. Coogan (1978) has identified chiastic patterns in verse 7ab, the verb "cease" opens verse 7a and closes 7b; in verse 19ab, the verb "fought" closes verse 19a and opens 19b; in verse 24ac the verse opens and closes with the verb "you are blessed." He also finds what he calls "full syntactic chiasmus." For example, in verse 13 ("went down"—"remnant"—"people of the LORD"—"went down"), verse 17ad (adverbial phrase "over Jordan"; verb "dwell"; adverbial phrase "on his landings"; verb "dwell").

j) We need not dwell here on the most common feature of Hebrew poetry, the use of parallelism in its many guises. A great deal has been written about the use of parallelism in Hebrew poetry, and Judges 5 represents most, if not all, forms of this basic poetic phenomenon. Suffice it to say that the most common form of parallelism in Judges 5 would seem to be that in which the second line of the form adds some new piece of information, thus raising the first line to a new height; for example, verse 3 "to the Lord . . . to the Lord the God of Israel;" verse 7b "arose . . . arose as a mother;" verse 23b "to the help of the Lord . . . to the help of the Lord against the mighty." This additional phrase describing or defining the action of the verb or of the noun phrase in the first half of the clause differs from the use of synonymous phrases in the second half of the parallel structure. The latter are merely different ways of expressing the same thought, whereas heightening parallelism repeats the phrase but adds some additional piece of information to complete the phrase. That this feature is not typical of narrative discourse is known and needs no further elaboration here.

The prose form in chapter 4 has one example of parallelism, a most unusual thing in prose. It is an example of "staircase parallelism" and is found in 4.18.

k) Figurative language is widely used in both prose and poetry, but used to a much greater degree in poetry. The Deborah song finds its place within the broad spectrum of Hebrew figurative expression. We can note at this juncture that often in poetry one finds the use of cosmic imagery, exactly the kind of imagery we find in 5.4-5.

Figurative imagery has with it certain associated ideas and meanings. For example, the cosmic imagery is associated with Yahweh's appearance. This may be in self-revelation as at Sinai (Exo 19), or in judgment (Psa 68.7-8), or in majesty (Psa 97.1-5). Use of the figure by the poet triggers all or some of those associations in the mind of the hearer to produce a richer or deeper meaning. The poet draws upon these implications or associations to enrich the impact of the words themselves.

In chapter 4 there is very little figurative expression. We have the expression "sold into the hands of" in verse 2, for example, but not a great deal of other language which we can label "figurative." In the poem, however, there is a much wider resort to figurative expression. Deborah is described as "a mother in Israel." Other examples can be found throughout, such as in verse 10, "you who ride on tawny asses . . . ," to indicate classes of citizens; verse 15 "they rushed forth at his heels," and so on.

From the above discussion we can appreciate that heightened language and expression, which is alleged to characterize poetic discourse, can be defined in part as the use of rare or coined terms, the use of the full range of the lexical dictionary available to the poet. We have seen that in its use of irony, of repetitions of verb and noun phrase, of word plays such as the name Deborah and the phrase *dabberi* (verse 12), that poetic form involves vocabulary and syntax which supports the creation of mood and atmosphere. Rather than simply conveying certain facts, the poet aims to entertain and stimulate the emotions in the process of passing on the basic message that the poem contains. We have seen also that the poem abbreviates expressions and omits information, calling the reader to expand on this terseness from knowledge of the wider cultural context, or from his or her imagination. Together with formal features such as parallelism and chiasmus, the poet resorts to the full literary range in his or her attempt to evoke, to suggest, to challenge the reader to feel and to sense, rather than to simply convey facts in a more mundane fashion. Poetry then operates on a level with a wide topographical range rather than on a generally flat plain. All of these distinctive features of poetry can be seen in a comparison of Judges 4 and 5.

The poet also uses rhythm, that is to say he or she presents material at different "speeds," at times hurrying over certain aspects of the presentation with terse and abbreviated style, and at others slowing down the action by the use of repetition and synonymous verbs. Judges 5 exemplifies this latter in a wonderful way in verses 24-27 as the poet relates the death of Sisera at the hands of Jael. This high point in the poem, this climax, is achieved artistically by virtually stopping the action, or at least describing the death of Sisera in slowly advancing "frames." In this way the reader/hearer has time to take in the scene in all its detail. As the climax to the battle, this slowing of the pace of the poem also serves to emphasize the final irony. Yahweh delivers Israel by the hand of a foreign woman. Poetic form and intent are brought together.

3. *The Poet and Imagination*

One of the more obvious differences between Judges 4 and 5 lies in the final section of chapter 5. Here the poet describes a scene in which Sisera's mother, together possibly with some of Sisera's harem, impatiently awaits his return. Although it is a highly likely occurrence (see Psa

68.12), the importance of this scene rests not on whether it took place or not, but in the poet's creative mind. This is the scene as he imagines it. With this scene the final irony, the ultimate rebuke of the enemy is presented. The poet, in giving this version of events, provides a scene from within a very fertile imagination. In doing so, we are reminded that poetry diverges from narrative in its freedom to create scenes that are generally within the realm of possibility, and that will enhance the overall atmosphere and purpose of the poem.

The narrator or storyteller may not feel the same kind of freedom to resort to imaginative creativity as the poet does, and to that extent we are witness to another major difference between story and poem. There may be other constraints on storytellers keeping them closer to a general outline of a known event, or to represent the "facts" of that event or situation with at least some closer attention to actuality. The poet, however, is under no such constraint. He or she can engage in imaginative addition as part of the overall brief to entertain as well as to preserve and pass on the tradition.

Poetry may legitimately diverge much further from "the facts" than story and narrative. This is a requirement of the form, or at least it is a characteristic of the form.

For the Bible translator, however, although these facts may be assented to, there is a further question. With the possibility of moving more into audio and other dramatic translations, the form in which the material must be cast to conform to the conventions of that medium will raise difficult questions about "faithfulness." If we use Judges 4 and 5 as a possible model, we must acknowledge that at times priority must be given to the requirements of the medium over that of the content. If creative imagination is a requirement of the form, then what happens to our criterion of "faithfulness" to the text? How can we be faithful to the text and to the medium at the same time? Both Judges 4 and 5 are quite some distance from the actual event they purport to describe. Neither one may be "faithful," defined in the narrowest sense, as records of that event. However, given that the poet can give almost free rein to imagination, within certain constraints such as probability, the poet can create a scene additional to what is in the base memory of the event and still be regarded as presenting a valid version of what took place. It is valid in terms of the purpose and function of the form, whether it be that of entertaining, of use in worship, or whatever other purpose the poetic form may be employed to represent.

4. Poetic Discourse and Translation

Because of the nature of poetic discourse, it may be asked whether this mode can be used to render all types of biblical material, or whether only certain kinds of material—those which lend themselves to this heightened form—are suitably transposed into poetic form.

In light of Judges 4 and 5, we might conclude that, if the story form recounting the battle and its gruesome end can be successfully cast in poetic form, then any other kind of material can also be so expressed. The question we need to consider is whether it is the content, or subject matter, which determines the appropriateness of the poetic form here. It is conceivable that in a given culture the idea of expressing the present battle scene as poetry could be a problem. Heightened language and "refinement" may be thought to go hand in hand, such that the topic of death on the battlefield is seen as the least appropriate candidate for poetic discourse. We are dealing here with the relationship between form and setting in the life of the community. Fixed forms are associated with one or more settings and are generally considered not to be used appropriately if found outside those settings. However, as far as the Deborah-Barak-Sisera-Jael episode is concerned, the Israelite tradition saw no problem about transposing the memory into poetic mode. In other words, the appropriateness of poetic form is probably determined on grounds other than that of subject matter. Cultural and linguistic sensibilities may be the major criterion for choosing one or the other mode of expression.

There are at least two factors which will be operative in a decision to attempt a poetic presentation of any piece of information. The one will be the appropriateness, within the particular cultural context and its oral or written literary tradition, of the poetic medium as the vehicle for conveying the material in question. Local cultural factors will have to be taken into account before a decision is made to render any discourse material in narrative or poetic form. What the cultural group considers can or should be rendered as poetry will vary from one group to another; certain subjects are appropriate to be thus expressed while others may not be. It is possible that what in Scripture is put into the poetic or prose mode would be more appropriately expressed in the opposite mode in the target culture. This cultural and traditional criterion may have more control over the form and its application than the subject-matter or content of a particular episode.

The second factor determining the possibility of using poetic form will be the skill of the individual translator. Translating into the poetic mode requires a literary sensitivity and an ability which not all speakers of a language possess. Not all have ready access to the entire range of its literary tools or are able to create neologisms at will, to handle chiasmus and parallelism. Not all are skilled at creating mood and atmosphere by their word pictures; not all can evoke and suggest in ways that hold the hearer's interest and lead to a creative use by the hearer of their own imagination. Regardless of the topic or the nature of the source language, a decision to render information or material as poetic will be influenced by the translator's literary skill in handling the higher literary forms of the mother tongue, his or her knowledge of the lexical range, of its "heightened" forms, and the like.

5. *Faithfulness in Poetic Transposition*

We have touched on the question of "faithfulness" briefly above but now need to give further thought to what the term might mean in this context. We note first that, when we are dealing with much of the biblical material, we are handling a text that has already passed through a longer or shorter period of oral transmission. During this process the storyteller or narrator seems to have had a degree of flexibility in how the material was narrated, depending upon the situation and circumstances under which the recounting took place. From the various doublets and repetitions in OT and NT, it would seem that ensuring that accounts conformed precisely in all details was not a concern of the biblical narrators and redactors. For this reason it is not proper to define "faithfulness" in too narrow a fashion; to do so may impose restrictions upon the material which are the concern of modern interpreters and translators but which were unknown and alien to the ancient world.

The oral materials now found in Scripture can be thought of as representing one isolated and "frozen" form in which the story or poem once occurred. Prior to the recital or record becoming fixed in the Scriptures, and even subsequently, in the oral circles that story would have been told and retold with many recognizably common elements, but almost certainly never in exactly the same form, with the same wording, or identical details. In the case of Judges 4 and 5 we are fortunate to have access to two different "frozen" forms of the Deborah incident. Both differ more or less from previous and subsequent oral recitals, yet we accept them as "faithful" records of the event in the broad sense. However, it is obvious that we cannot apply the criterion of "faithfulness" in the same way to both Judges 4 and 5 without stretching our understanding of the concept. Perhaps we apply the notion of "faithfulness" to these two accounts simply because they both are found in the Scriptures, and because we are unclear about what we mean when we use the concept "faithfulness." We still have to ask, "faithful to what?" If we found such divergent accounts elsewhere than in the Scriptures, we might simply take them as two different accounts, one of which was "correct" and the other "less correct" in terms of their representation of what might have actually happened. An alternative would be to try to level the two and make light of their differences for the sake of a preconceived notion about the nature of the Scriptures, denying the possibility of there being variant and even conflicting accounts of the one incident.

The discrepancies we have noted above between Judges 4 and 5 raise the question of the relationship between the two. Is one prior to and closer to telling what actually happened than the other? Is chapter 4 a "prosaic reduction" dependent upon chapter 5, or is chapter 5 a "poetic expansion" of chapter 4? Are both accounts simply different versions of a common memory told from variant perspectives? In view of the fact that both are the result of some period of oral reporting and recital, it makes good sense to approach them as two versions of what originally was a common memory. Each version will have had its own origin, history and functional setting. What this means, of course, is that there is no way in which we can give any final answer to the question about which might more closely approximate what actually transpired on the battlefield when the Israelite army encountered Sisera's troops.

The translator's concern with faithfulness in rendering the text's meaning is expressed in the attempt to faithfully transfer the meaning of a text that is a "faithful" record of an original event or situation. However, that record is "faithful" in a very different sense than the translation is "faithful." It raises the prior question of whether what we are to translate is actually faithful in the sense of "accurate," as an account of what took place. The question of "historicity" is an important element in the discussion of "faithfulness," even if it is not one which impinges so directly or consciously on the translator's task. The translator needs to acknowledge that what he or she struggles to render "faithfully" will not necessarily be faithful in the sense of being absolutely accurate as a record of the actual circumstances of the event or situation being portrayed. In other words "faithfulness" applied to the translator's brief ignores the prior question of the "faithfulness" of the biblical record itself. We simply take the text as it presently stands and seek to render it in a manner which is faithful.

In the likely event that both Judges 4 and 5 stem from some common memory, how can these two divergent records help us to define "faithfulness" in translation? Perhaps we can think of it on two levels: the first would be the need to be faithful to the message; the second would be faithfulness to the form, not of the source form necessarily, but of the target form.

a) *Faithfulness to the "original message."* I use the term "original message" rather loosely for the sake of convenience, as we are all aware that oral recital of stories and such are actually a dialogue between the storyteller, the material, and the audience. This dynamic setting means that the "original message" is problematic to define, for the recital was never exactly the same on every occasion of its recital. In the case of a poetic representation, the "original" is generally further removed from the event than is a prose account. However, here I use the phrase to refer to *the message which the present frozen account purports to convey* within its current biblical setting.

Translators are required to determine to the best of considered scholarly opinion what that message is, what is the purpose and meaning of the text. Then they are to translate in such a way as to preserve that source message in all its nuances and emphases, but at the same time to communicate it through the medium of the receptor form and language.

b) *Faithfulness to the form.* By "form" here, I refer to the form in which the target audience is being presented with the message derived from the source text.

As has been suggested above, virtually any piece of literature can be rendered in poetic form. The particular content or field of reference of the material concerned is probably not at issue. So long as the target community is able to accept the poetic form as the appropriate one in which to present material, the translator is free to use that form. This will apply regardless of the source language form. If the poetic form is chosen as the appropriate target form, then the translator has to be "faithful" to all the dictates and requirements of that form, while at the same time being "faithful" to the essential message of the source material, regardless of the form in which it might have appeared.

However, in attempting to meet the requirements of faithfulness to both the message and the form, a tension inevitably arises. Leaving aside the question of whether one should use alien OT or NT forms within the receptor language (RL), it is obvious that, in being faithful to the RL form chosen, we will often be forced to modify at least some of the features of the source language text. The peculiar literary features of the source language cannot be imported entirely into the receptor language form without doing violence to that form. Furthermore, if in terms of form the RL demands certain features be present, we must incorporate these even if not in the original Hebrew or Greek text. Likewise the form may require the omission of certain source language features. Our only way forward is to try to ensure that the basic overall message of the source is carried across into the RL, while at the same time meeting all of the RL's formal demands.

Yet we shall no doubt have to recognize and deal with the fact that churches and review committees will almost certainly reject a printed translation which follows fully the dictates of the RL form if the resultant translation departs from a revered and ancient translation or version. We may not like it for this to be so, but the fact remains that church audiences are notoriously conservative. Perhaps the transposition of a text into the dramatic or audio format will be able to escape this problem to some extent, for those media generally will not be viewed as "real Scripture," so different standards will be applied. However, for the translator charged with the task of rendering the source language text into a variant form in the RL, regardless of the medium chosen, the translation will have to conform to all the requirements of the form, yet retain the *overall* message of the original. If we cannot in good conscience accept that a "faithful" poetic (or audio/video) rendering will have to accommodate fully to the receptor language form, then perhaps we should not engage in such translations.

References

Alter, R. 1981. *The Art of Biblical Narrative*. London and Sydney: George Allen and Unwin.

———. 1985. *The Art of Biblical Poetry*. New York: Basic Books Inc.

Coogan, M.D. 1978. "A Structural Analysis of the Song of Deborah." *Catholic Biblical Quarterly* 40: 143-166.

Follis, E.R. 1987. *Directions in Biblical Hebrew Poetry*. JSOT Supplement 40. Sheffield: JSOT Press.

Freedman, D.N. 1975. "Early Israelite History in the Light of Early Israelite Poetry." In H. Goedicke and J.J.M. Roberts, editors, *Unity and Diversity: Essays in the History, Literature, and Religion of the Ancient Near East*, 3-35. Baltimore and London: Johns Hopkins University Press.

Hauser, A.J. 1987. "Two Songs of Victory: A Comparison of Exodus 15 and Judges 5." In E.R. Follis, editor, *Directions in Biblical Hebrew Poetry*, pages 265-284. JSOT Supplement 40. Sheffield: JSOT Press.

Kugel, J.L. 1981. *The Idea of Biblical Poetry: Parallelism and Its History*. New Haven: Yale University Press.

Watson, W.G.E. 1986. *Classical Hebrew Poetry: A Guide to its Techniques*. JSOT Supplement 26. Sheffield: JSOT Press.

Webb, B.G. 1987. *The Book of Judges: An Integrated Reading*. JSOT Supplement 46. Sheffield: JSOT Press.

The Song of the Vineyard: Love Lyric or Comic Ode? A Study of the Oral and Discourse Features of Isaiah 5.1-7

David J. Clark

Introduction

This short section (Isa 5.1-7) is clearly a self-contained discourse unit distinguished in both form and content from the passages which surround it. It is set out in poetic format in *Biblia Hebraica Stuttgartensia,* which seems a reasonable decision, since it claims to be a song (5.1). This claim implies both that it is some sort of poetry (we need not enter the debate about what constitutes Hebrew poetry), and that it was originally intended for oral delivery, with the written record being secondary. A song it may be, yet in many respects it is not comparable with the Psalms. They were indeed intended for oral delivery, but in a cultic, often liturgical context. The Song of the Vineyard was not apparently intended for cultic use, and its purpose is sociopolitical rather than devotional. In that sense it is more readily comparable with Jotham's parable (Judges 9.8-15) or Nathan's parable (2 Sam 12.1-4) than with a psalm.[1] It is the purpose of this article to examine the oral and discourse features of Isa 5.1-7 with a view to clarifying the structure of the poem and trying to evaluate some of the possible impact on its oral translation. A romanized transcription and interlinear translation follow.

1. *'ashirah nna' lididi | shirath dodi lekarmo /* 1-6
let-me-sing ptc.for-my-beloved song-of my-love for-his-vineyard

kerem hayah lididi beqeren ben-shamen // 2-5
vineyard (there-)was for-my-beloved on-hill son-of-oil

2. *waye‘azzeqehu wayesaqqelehu wayyitta‘ehu soreq* | *3-4*
and-he-digged-it and-he-destoned-it and-he-planted-it best-vine

wayyiven migdal bethoko | *4-3*
and-he-built tower in-its-midst

wegam-yeqev chatsev bo / *5-3*
and-even-wine-vat he-dug in-it

wayeqaw la‘asoth ‘anavim wayya‘as be’ushim // *6-5*
and-he-looked to-make grapes and-it-made sour-grapes

3. *we‘attah yoshev yerushalayim we’ish yehudah* / *7-5*
and-now inhabitant-of Jerusalem and-man-of Judah

shifetu-na’ | *beni uven karmi* // *8-4*
you-pl.-judge-ptc. between-me and-between my-vineyard

4. *mah-lla‘asoth ‘od lekarmi* | *9-3*
what-to-do more for-my-vineyard

welo’ ‘asithi bo / *10-3*
and-not I-have-done in-it?

maddua‘ qiwwethi la‘asoth ‘anavim wayya‘as be’ushim // *11-6*
why I-looked to-make grapes and-it-made sour-grapes?

5. *we‘attah ’odi‘a-nna’ ’ethekem* |
and-now I-will-cause-to-know-ptc. you-pl.-emph.

’eth ’asher-’ani ‘oseh lekarmi / *12-7*
obj. which-I-emph. about-to-do to-my-vineyard

haser mesukkatho wehayah leva‘er | *13-4*
to-remove its-hedge and-it-shall-become to-be-devoured

parots gedero wehayah lemirmas // *14-4*
to-break-down its-wall and-it-shall-become to-be-trampled

6. *wa'ashithehu bathah*
and-I-will-place-it ruin

lo' yizzamer welo' ye'ader | 15-6
not it-shall-be-pruned and-not it-shall-be-hoed

we'alah shamir washayith / 16-3
and-will-come-up brier and-thorn

we'al he'avim 'atsawweh |
and-upon the-clouds I-will-command

mehamtir 'alayw matar // 17-6
from-to-rain upon-it rain

7. *ki kerem* YHWH *tseva'oth beth yisra'el* | 18-6
for vineyard-of LORD-of hosts house-of Israel

we'ish yehudah neta' sha'ashu'ayw / 19-4
and-man-of Judah plant-of his-delight

wayeqaw lemishpat wehinneh mispach |
and-he-looked for-justice and-behold bloodshed

litsedaqah wehinneh tse'aqah // 20-7
for-righteousness and-behold scream

In the above transcription, // represents *silluq*, / represents *athnach*, and | represents *zaqef parvum*. Verse numbers are at the left and line numbers at the right, together with the number of accented syllables in each line (following the hyphen).

Analysis of Isaiah 5.1-7

There is not a very close connection with the preceding material. The unit begins with no narrative setting other than the first line, and the reader or hearer has to infer the context from this opening sentence. (It will be argued below that this line is best understood as not being part of the song proper.) It must be assumed that the prophet has an audience, and the audience presumably starts by assuming that the singer is the prophet speaking in his own persona; only later does it become explicit that he is speaking as YHWH's representative. The presence of the audience is made explicit in verse 3 when they are addressed with a vocative expression. Verse 3 also sees a change of the persona speaking, though this is made explicit in Hebrew only in a low-key way by a change of pronoun to first person. The words in verses 3 to 6 are the words of the owner of the vineyard, though we assume that they too are reported by the prophet and delivered by him on the owner's behalf. The same speaker continues to speak, but wearing, so to say, a different hat. It is only at the end of verse 6 that the audience can discern that the owner is YHWH, and this is immediately confirmed in verse 7, which is the prophet's closing comment (resuming his own persona) and the climax of the whole unit. There is thus an inclusio in terms of the speakers: the prophet in verses 1-2 and 7, and the owner in verses 3-6. By giving more weight to the pause that seems to be implied between verses 4 and 5, one might also analyze this as a chiasmus: prophet (1-2): owner (3-4) :: owner (5-6): prophet (7).

We look now in more detail at the Hebrew text, verse by verse. English renderings are from RSV unless otherwise stated. In verse 1a there is a first person introduction, the words of the prophet, which stands outside the poem proper. We note the particle *nna'* attached to the verb translated "sing"; this is repeated with the verbs translated "judge" in verse 3 and "tell" in verse 5, though only in verse 3 does it have any representation in RSV ("I pray you"), and this is dropped from NRSV. Its occurrence here at the beginning of the discourse suggests that it has some function at the discourse level as an opening marker; if this is so, then in verses 3 and 5 it could be interpreted as helping to mark the onset of a new (sub)unit, though in neither case does the establishment of a new (sub)unit depend on the occurrence of the particle. The identity of "my beloved" is not made explicit at this point, though at the second occurrence it becomes clear that the "beloved" is the owner of the vineyard. In verse 1b we come to a third person description that initiates the allegory. We may compare the words *kerem hayah* (literally "there was a vineyard") with *shene 'anashim hayu* ("There were two men") in 2 Sam 12.1 as a typical story-opening structure. This is where the parable proper begins.

Also in verse 1, but more on the level of orality, we may note the cognation, or "root echoes," between the words translated "sing" and "song," and between those translated "beloved" and "love (song)." In English the former is reproduced quite naturally, but the latter sounds rather clumsy, though presumably it did not have this effect in Hebrew. The last words of the verse, translated "on a very fertile hill" in RSV are literally "on a horn the son of oil." This double trope (horn = hill, son of oil = fertile) fits Hebrew patterns of figurative speech but is alien to the point of meaninglessness in English. Even a literal translation like RSV rightly makes no attempt to preserve it. But some impact is lost when the figures are simply replaced by plain language, and this must weaken the effectiveness of the translation in comparison with the original.

In verse 2 the third person description continues, and the picture which forms the allegory is brought to completion. The first three words in Hebrew are verbs with identical prefixes and suffixes, giving an assonance with a pounding rhythm, as well as alliteration between the first two verbs. The word *soreq* refers to a high-quality vine and as such would have carried an emotive impact that is bound to be lost in English, and indeed in any social setting where viticulture is not a central feature of life. The word rendered "wine vat" is marked in Hebrew in two ways: it is front-shifted in its clause, and it is preceded by the particle *gam*. The effect is to bring it into focus and draw attention to it; it appears that the effort of building a wine vat in advance was a public display of the owner's confidence that the fruit of the vineyard would be good. In the final line the Hebrew has a pair of antonyms which RSV translates "grapes" and "wild grapes." The fact that English does not have such a pair of unit terms leads to the awkward asymmetry of contrasting an unqualified noun with the same noun plus an adjective. The balance can easily be restored by using antonymous adjectives to maintain the contrast; for instance, "sweet grapes" and "sour grapes" (compare NJB "fine grapes" and "wild grapes," REB "choice grapes" and "wild grapes"). One should perhaps note that the English expression "sour grapes" has acquired, probably ultimately from Aesop, proverbial overtones that the Hebrew does not have. This is not entirely unwelcome in a passage with a didactic purpose; it resonates with indigenous English gnomic wisdom.

Verse 3 opens a new unit of the discourse, which is marked both by the occurrence of the adverb *we'attah* "now" (repeated in verse 5) and by a double vocative ("O inhabitants of Jerusalem and men of Judah").

Although English versions translate these vocatives as plural, they are actually both singular in Hebrew. Though they are no doubt collective in intent, so that a plural in English is quite appropriate, perhaps the Hebrew singulars added a touch of immediacy and personal appeal to the original oral delivery. The main verb "judge" is emphasized by the particle *na'* (compare verses 1 and 5) and is given further prominence by the presence of the Hebrew punctuation mark called *zaqef parvum* in *Biblia Hebraica Stuttgartensia.* This makes it the shortest punctuation unit in the poem, and indeed the only such unit consisting of a single word. As mentioned in connection with verse 1, although the particle *nna'/na'* occurs in verses 1, 3, and 5, RSV translates it only here in verse 3 ("I pray you"). It is not clear what conditions the absence of the *dagesh forte* from *na'* in this occurrence. It does not appear to be the presence or absence of *maqqef,* which is absent from verse 1 but present in verse 5, both of which have the *dagesh forte.* We may note that the vowel preceding *(n)na'* is *a* in verses 1 and 5, but *u* in verse 3, but there is no obvious reason why this should affect the doubling of the consonant. Whatever the conditioning factor may be, presumably the doubling or lack of it had some emotive effect in an oral delivery.

Verse 4 continues in the first person with two questions to the audience which have a strong emotive impact; they may be taken as rhetorical in that the answers to them are clearly implied in the previous verses, but in the setting of interplay between prophet and audience, they probably invite the listeners to verbalize their response. It is interesting to observe that a *dagesh forte* follows an *a* vowel and a *maqqef* in the opening words *mah-lla'asoth.* The root *'-s-h* occurs three times, the second and third occurrences as part of the exact repetition of the last four words of verse 2, which includes the antonym pair. The root *q-w-h* is echoed from verse 2 (also in verse 7). This repetition serves to magnify the owner's sense of disappointment at the failure of the crop. One may also note that the syntactic and semantic structures are slightly at variance in the last line. The interrogative *maddua'* "why" is syntactically linked with the verb *qiwwethi* "looked for" but must be taken semantically with the verb *wayya'as* "yielded." The question is not why the owner looked for good fruit, but why the vineyard did not produce it. Since the prophet could perfectly well have put the interrogative with the second verb, its displacement must be seen as a poetic device that momentarily delays the hearer's or reader's interpretive process and further reinforces the disappointment.

Before verse 5 we assume an interval in which the members of the audience discuss the questions posed in verse 4 and give their answers. This event is not stated but can be inferred from the context. That there is a relatively major break between verses 4 and 5 is marked by the occurrence of *we'attah* "now" (compare verse 3) and the repetition of the particle *nna'* (compare verses 1 and 3). The use of the emphatic object pronoun *'ethekem* "you" highlights the contrast with verse 3, where the audience was invited to express a judgment, but now is invited, or even commanded, to listen to the owner's judgment. There is a further echo of the root *'-s-h,* which has occurred several times in verses 2 and 4. The second half of verse 5 introduces new vocabulary and describes the punishment of the vineyard, the opposite process to its loving construction in verse 2. Of the four clauses of this half of the verse, the first two and the last two are syntactically and morphologically parallel with each other, giving an obvious rhythmic balance.

Verse 6 continues with the same speaker and adds further details to the description of the punishment. The syntax is not parallel with the last half of verse 5, though there is some internal parallelism of structure within verse 6. The first verb is generic and is followed by four specifics, two grammatically negative and two grammatically positive (though psychologically negative). The first line shows assonance between the verbs *yizzamer* and *ye'ader*. The first and third lines contain the partially alliterative roots (*z-m-r* and *m-t-r,*) and the latter is followed by a cognate noun that echoes and reinforces the alliteration. The second line displays a measure of both alliteration and assonance in the words *shamir washayith*. In the final clause the object "clouds" is front-shifted to occur before its governing verb "command," to bring it into an emphatic position. This emphasis contributes to the unexpectedness of the statement of which it is part, and this element of surprise is instrumental in revealing by implication that the owner of the vineyard is YHWH himself. Who else could command the clouds?

In verse 7 the discourse is again in the third person, and the prophet resumes his role as speaker. This is not made explicit and has to be inferred from the reference to YHWH in the third person. The opening word *ki* "for" binds this verse to the whole of the preceding discourse, of which it is the interpretation and climax. The repetition of *kerem* picks up the *kerem* at the opening of the song in verse 1, and the root *n-t-'* is also an echo of the same root in verse 2. The first two cola exhibit a chiasmus (subject : complement :: complement : subject). In the second complement, *we'ish yehudah* repeats the same phrase as in the vocative in verse 3. The final dénouement of the last line is linked with the original allegory by the repetition of the verb *wayeqaw* from verse 2 (RSV "looked for"; compare verse 4). This verb governs two pairs of objects but is left implicit before the second pair. The second half of verse 7 is the most artfully contrived part of the whole discourse, containing a double word play with two pairs of antonymous alliterations (*mishpat* and *mispach, tsedaqah* and *tse'aqah*). This is the climax of the pericope, echoing the use of antonyms in verses 2 and 4.

We may next sum up the analysis, referring to the text now, not by the verse numbers on the left hand side in the display above, but by the numbers of the lines on the right, preceding the hyphen. Lines 2-6 and 7-11 form stanzas delimited by discourse markers, and balancing each other especially in the repetition of thought in lines 6 and 11. The inclusion of line 1 would ruin the stanza structure, and it is better regarded as not being part of the poem proper. Lines 2-11 also display a rhythmic balance in the number of accented syllables in their constituent cola. The cola are delimited according to the following axioms: every occurrence of *silluq* and *athnach* in the Masoretic punctuation is taken to mark a colon break; occurrences of *zaqef parvum* are counted as a colon break unless the resulting unit would not contain at least one finite verb, and thus would not be a fully formed clause. The accented syllables are indicated by the number at the right hand side of the text above, following the hyphen. This scheme yields the following count over lines 2-11: 54335:54336; only an extra beat in the final line disturbs the parallelism, probably deliberately. The rhythmic pattern thus matches the semantic content, being parallelistic and repetitive. Any attempt to include line 1 in this rhythmic pattern simply wrecks it, giving further support to the view that line 1 stands apart from the poem as its introduction.

The major break in the poem, indicated both by discourse markers and a change of the speaker's persona, comes at line 12, and there is a complex balance of semantic and rhythmic factors in lines 12-20. The overall syllable count calculated according to the above scheme is 744-636-647, almost a chiastic balance. Semantically lines 12-17 (744-636) go together as the words of the owner of the vineyard, with lines 18-20 (647) separate as the words of the prophet. Rhythmically, however, there seems to be something very close to an inverse balance between lines 12-14 and 18-20 (744 against 647): a longer line in the second unit.

Rhythmic considerations may thus explain why the word *wayeqaw* occurs only once in the last colon. Syntactically it could perfectly well have been repeated before *litsedaqah,* and rhetorically there could be added force in doing so. But in fact, although the repetition is semantically essential, the technique of gapping is employed, and the second occurrence is left implicit. To make it explicit would destroy the rhythmic structure. Lines 15-17 can be analyzed as 636, with a short and rhythmically climactic line in the middle. Thus the semantic and rhythmic factors moderate and counterbalance each other in this half of the poem.

We may now examine some of the semantic subtleties of the poem, which involve several reversals of expectation. Indeed the whole poem might be characterized as a discourse-level paradox. The prophet labels his poem as a *shirath dodi,* rendered by RSV as "a love song." This expression in English is misleading in so far as it implies a song about human love between a man and a woman, whereas in fact there is nothing in the poem that is amatory or contains any identifiable sexual or erotic allusions. But it does at least suggest that the content of the song is positive about its subject, and this is a fair reflection of the Hebrew. The GNB rendering "a song of my friend (and his vineyard)" hints at a positive content while avoiding amatory implications, but it is disappointingly bland. Despite its positive label, however, the song at the end turns out to convey a sharp and bitter denunciation, so that there is a reversal of expectation on the macrolevel. Within the song there is a clear and explicit reversal of expectation on the part of the owner of the vineyard in line 6, repeated in line 11. The owner had taken every step necessary to ensure a crop of good grapes, but the vintage nevertheless proved worthless.

Lines 12-16 contain a further, and perhaps crucial, reversal of expectation. If the situation described had occurred in real life, the owner might be expected to dig up the vine and replant with different stock, but in this case the owner decides to write off his entire investment of capital and labor by destroying the vineyard. This is such a bizarre and self-defeating overreaction that one wonders whether it is an example of almost slapstick comedy—Isaiah's hitherto unsuspected version of an Irish joke? If the audience was indeed reduced to laughter at this point, then the revelation in line 17, that the owner of the vineyard is none other than YHWH (which is itself a further reversal of expectation), would come with even stronger force: how could YHWH of all people be so stupid? In lines 18 and 19 the vineyard is identified as the audience (another surprise), and the allegory is interpreted in ethical terms in line 20. The absurdity of the vineyard's treatment in lines 13-16 underlines the severity of the punishment implied by the condemnation in line 20. This leads easily into the series of oracles of doom that take up Isaiah 5.8-30, though there is no structural similarity with them.

Implications for Translation

Although the identification of structural discourse features and their effects is relatively straightforward, it is much harder to assess the effect of those items tentatively identified in the above analysis as features of orality, since there are no native speakers of eighth century Hebrew extant. If more such observations were made on other sections of text, it might become more feasible to draw some conclusions, but for the present they seem to be beyond a firm grasp. However, there is no doubt that translators need to take account of the issues raised by discourse analysis in preparing their drafts, and to consider a number of thorny questions. Is it possible for structural features of the original text to be carried over into another language? To what extent should they be carried over even if it is possible? What about points of emphasis and thematic focus? Are the normal ways of indicating emphasis and/or focus in the receptor language compatible with the retention of structural features from the original language? How can the aesthetic value and emotive impact of the original be conveyed in a translation? Can format and typographical ingenuity be used to reflect the discourse structure of the original more clearly without simply mystifying the modern reader? We will now attempt to initiate a discussion of some of these issues in connection with Isaiah 5.1-7, though a comprehensive treatment is beyond the scope of this paper.

A significant decision for the whole poem is taken in the choice of terms for the rendering of the genre-defining words *shirath dodi*. As mentioned above, the English term "love song" is quite out of keeping with the content, especially if verses 5-6 are taken to be a humorous lampoon of anything the owner of a vineyard would ever do in real life. It may conjure up notions of a sentimental Victorian ballad but certainly does not prepare the reader for a comical discussion of viticultural economics, with an ethical sting in the tail! If this is what the poem really is (and I am not certain myself, but will take it as a working hypothesis), then a more appropriate term in English might be "friendly ditty." "Ditty" has humorous, rather low-level overtones that might at first seem shocking in the context of Scripture, but does it not have a certain appropriateness in a setting where the prophet has to engage and hold the attention of a very worldly-minded group of people who know a lot more about the realities of vineyards than a modern English audience? Another possible term in English might be "ode," which can have a low-level meaning but does not necessarily do so, and thus might seem more appropriate in Scripture. It does not, however, collocate well with "friendly." Maybe the clash between the introduction and the final line could be accommodated by the label "cheery ode."

The next issue lies in the emotive effect of the topic of the poem, namely a vineyard. In a society where wine is a central feature of the culture, a vineyard will have a strong, clear, and well-understood emotive impact on hearers or readers. This would be the case in most southern European societies and languages. But with the possible exception of parts of Australia, South Africa, or California, it is not the case in the English-speaking world and would certainly not be the case in many other language areas. Ought one therefore to make a cultural adjustment in order to maintain equivalence of emotive effect in the topic? The translation principles advocated by the Bible Societies would here bring into play respect for the original culture and would reject the idea of such an adjustment. The most that might be permitted would be a more generic term such as "orchard." This remains in the semantic domain of fruit cultivation, and has positive connotations for English speakers, so it might be acceptable in some contexts. However, in the light of the detailed description of the construction of the vineyard which follows in verse 2, such a course is not practical in this case. The translator into English has to accept that there is an irremediable loss of impact at this level of cultural relevance.

More emotive effect is lost by the elimination of the Hebrew tropes in line 2. Anything approaching a literal translation would be ludicrous; perhaps the most that can be done to redeem the situation is to use a mildly metonymic term like "slope," which has some association with vineyards, in place of the bland word "hill."

The features of assonance, alliteration, and pounding rhythm in verse 2 raise questions of translational equivalence on the phonological level. It might be possible to contrive some English rendering that embodied roughly parallel features, but it is unlikely that they would have a similar effect on the reader (or in this case, the hearer) that the original had, if only because we do not know what effect the original did have. But this raises the broader question of what aspects of present-day usage in the receptor language indicate poetry, and how, if at all, they should be used in a translation. Rhyme is a traditional feature of English poetry but is not very fashionable at the moment among serious poets. It is still employed in humorous pieces such as limericks, jingles for TV advertisements, and so on, and if the interpretation of verses 5-6 as humorous is accepted, then rhyme might be deemed appropriate at least for verses 1b-6. If this interpretation is rejected, however, rhyme would probably not be considered appropriate. Effective use of rhyme usually requires a regular meter, so that a decision about rhyme will affect more than just the choice of lexical items that offer rhyming syllables; it will also constrain line length and perhaps the number of lines required.

The issue of focus arises in connection with the mention of the press for treading the grapes in line 5. It is marked by front-shifting and by an emphatic particle. Both these devices are available in English, and with apparently similar effect, but would they both be needed together? Perhaps either one would suffice alone. It is interesting to note that, with the noble exception of New Jewish Version (NJV), major English versions have ignored this matter. Even NJV has neglected the similar focus marking of the clouds in line 17. There GNB is the version to make an effort, but it ends up marking the verb "forbid" rather than the clouds.

In verse 3 the change of identity in the persona of the speaker is not explicitly marked in Hebrew. The question therefore arises whether it should be more clearly marked in English. GNB is the only major version which is bold enough to do so, with the words "So now my friend says." This is quite helpful at the denotational level but to some extent interrupts the flow of the poem. If the poem proper (verses 1b-7) has been put inside quotation marks, one might perhaps begin a second-degree quote at verse 3. This would alert the reader (but not the hearer unless a different voice is used) that some change is taking place, but would not specify its nature. Also in verse 3 the imperative verb "judge" is in focus, but it is hard in English to do other than bring the subject into special focus, though after the long vocative phrases in line 7, this is probably not out of place. JB and NJB have "I ask you to judge," which achieves an appropriate emphasis, but perhaps NJV "you be the judges" is best. In verse 4 the displacement of the interrogative "why?" is not maintained in any major English version, and it is difficult to see that it would have any affect other than momentary confusion if it were.

The relatively major break before verse 5 might be indicated by an extra blank line, though this device could pass unnoticed by many readers. The choice of the emphatic pronoun *'ethekem* in line 12 seems to deserve some representation in English; the difficulty is that a pronoun in this context would usually be emphasized by means of intonation, and that is not indicated in the script, so that it is not easy to determine how far major English versions have allowed for it. This might be a place where the use of italics for the pronoun would help the reader to sense the emphasis of the original.

In verse 6 there would be little hope of reproducing alliteration in another language, and the impact of alliteration might in any case be quite different from that in Hebrew. Some effort should however be made to retain the focus on "clouds," though no major English version does so.

The chiasmus in verse 7 may be formally retained, but its effect may not be the same in other languages. In English many readers would probably fail to notice it, and some may even find it confusing. The antonyms at the end of the verse would have to be reproduced, but the possibility of keeping the alliteration is low, and its desirability would depend on the way alliteration is used in the receptor language. In English it would probably sound rather corny. However, rhyme may be appropriate here at the climax of the poem even if it is not employed elsewhere. And since Isaiah was himself lexically constrained by the alliteration in the Hebrew, perhaps the modern translator can award himself some compensating lexical liberty in attaining a comparable phonological effect.

Translation

This section presents three English renderings, the first two adaptations of two different English translations, RSV and GNB, in the light of the above analysis. The adaptations retain the wording of these versions as far as possible and make alterations only where the analysis suggests that something closer to the impact of the original text might be attained, or where the result sounds closer to spoken English. The third version is the author's and attempts to incorporate some of the virtues of both the others. However, a truly poetic rendering, either serious or comic, is beyond the bardic prowess of the present writer!

Based on RSV

1. Let me sing for my beloved a song of love about his vineyard.
   My beloved had a vineyard on a very fertile slope.
2. He dug it and he cleared it and he planted choicest vines.
   He built a watchtower in its midst, and even a vat for wine.
   He looked for it to yield sweet grapes, but all its grapes were sour.

3. Now, Jerusalem's inhabitants, and citizens of Judah,
   you be the judges between me and my vineyard!
4. Was there anything more in the vineyard that I should have done?
   Why then when I looked for sweet grapes, were all its grapes so sour?

5. Now let me tell you what I'm going to do to that vineyard of mine:
   remove its hedge, and let it be destroyed!
   Break down its wall and let it be trampled on!
6. I'll make it a ruin, with no one to prune it and no one to hoe it,
   and briers and thorns will flourish there.
   Even the clouds I will forbid to let rain fall upon it!

7. For the LORD of Hosts' vineyard is the house of Israel!
   The people of Judah are his delightful plants!
   Where he looked for justice, behold only blood-lust is!
   In place of true compassion, behold nought but oppression!

Based on GNB

1. Now let me sing you this song, a song of my friend and his vineyard.
   My friend had a vineyard on a very fertile hill.
2. He dug the soil and cleared the stones, and planted finest vines.
   He built a tower to guard them, and even a pit to tread the grapes
   he excavated there.
   He waited for sweet grapes to form, but every grape was sour.
3. So now my friend says,
   "You people who live in Jerusalem and Judah,
   You judge between my vineyard and me.
4. Is there anything I failed to do for it? Were my hopes unfair?
   Then why did no sweet grapes form, but every grape was sour?

5. So now let me tell you what I am going to do to that vineyard of mine,
I'll take away the hedge and break down the wall around it,
so that animals can graze it and trample it down.
6. I won't trim the vines or hoe the ground.
It will be overgrown with briers and thorns.
Even the clouds I'll forbid to let rain fall upon it."

7. The LORD Almighty's vineyard is the people of Israel!
The people of Judah are the splendid vines he planted!
He waited for them to do good,
but all they did was shed blood!
He waited for them to do what was right,
But their victims cried out in fright!

Author's Own

1. Now let me sing for my friend a friendly song about his vineyard.
"My friend had a vineyard on a very fertile slope.
2. He dug it up and cleared the stones and planted finest vines.
He built a tower to guard it,
and even a winepress he hewed from the rock.
He hoped for it to grow sweet grapes, but all its grapes were sour!

3. " 'Now you, inhabitants of Jerusalem and citizens of Judah,
you be the ones to judge between me and my vineyard.
4. What more could I have done for my vineyard?
I hoped for it to grow sweet grapes, so why were they all sour?

5. " 'Now then let me tell you what I shall do to my vineyard:
I'll destroy the hedge and let beasts in to graze!
I'll break down the wall and let them trample round!
6. I'll let it go to ruin, with no one to prune it or hoe it—
it'll be taken over by briers and thorns!
Even the clouds I will forbid to let rain fall upon it!'

7. "For the vineyard of the Lord Almighty is the people of Israel!
The citizens of Judah are his delightful plants!
He hoped for them to do the right,

and found instead the rule of might!
He hoped for firm integrity,
and found but deep iniquity!"

Note

1. It is interesting to observe scholarly ambivalence about the poetic status of these passages: BHS prints both in poetic format, as do JB and NJB, whereas NEB and REB print neither as poetry. RSV printed neither as poetry, whereas NRSV prints as poetry the former but not the latter.

Anatomy of a Poem: Lamentations 1

By William D. Reyburn

The title of this article suggests dissecting Lamentations chapter 1 to ascertain its parts. While an operation to separate the various components that make up the poem is a valid undertaking, the purpose of anatomical explorations goes much further than merely taking things apart. The sense taken here is that given in Webster's New Collegiate dictionary: "The art of separating the parts of an animal or plant in order to ascertain their position, relations, structure, and function." Regardless of what metaphor is used as an aid to analysis and no matter how a poem is separated into its parts, the poem functions as a meaningful whole to convey its message. Nevertheless an examination of the elements of a poem and their relations to each other can assist the reader in gaining a better perspective of the ways in which the entire poem expresses its various levels of meaning.

Although chapter 1 of Lamentations is the subject of this article, it is necessary to make clear that separating chapter 1 from the rest of the poem creates something of a distortion. Chapter 1 is an integral part of the structure of the poem. For example, the five chapters of Lamentations may be viewed as a single chiastic configuration in which chapters 1 and 5 "are general summaries that show a greater psychic distance from events than the grim and pitiable scenes of death and destruction that are vividly drawn in chapters 2 and 4. Chapter 3, with its intensified acrostic form, complexly splices the lamenting voices of a number of 'I' speakers alongside the national 'we,' in order to build a subtle but powerful theological statement about the need for Israel to wait patiently on God's eventual decision to show mercy to the community."[1]

From half-line to verse

The smallest structural feature of this poem is the "half-line." Each pair of half-lines forms a line. Three lines combine to form a verse, except verse 7, which contains four lines. Editions of the Hebrew Bible print the poem in this way. Two half-lines are frequently structurally and/or semantically parallel. The beginning of each verse is identified by the next letter in the Hebrew alphabet so that the twenty-two letters of the alphabet mark the twenty-two verses of the poem.

Using the notation of James Kugel we may display the half-line, line, and verse arrangement as follows:

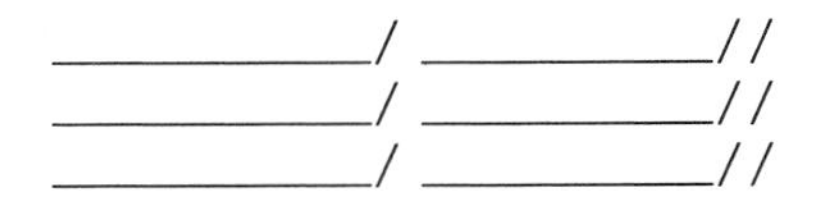

This notation is to be read as a verse consisting of three lines. Each line has two half-lines, each half-line being a clause. The pause between the half-lines is normally shorter than the pause at the end of the line.

From verse to strophe to stanza

The terminology used for speaking of the parts of a poem such as hemistich, colon, bicolon, and so forth is replaced in this article by half-lines, lines, and verses. Verses are grouped into strophes and strophes into stanzas. Verses that combine to form strophes have some shared structural and/or semantic/thematic features. To label a group of verses a strophe is to recognize that there is some kind of juncture between them. A break between two or more sets of strophes creates a still larger segmentation of the poem into discourse units that are here labeled

---

[1] Gottwald (1985), page 542.

stanzas. Two or more stanzas make up the poem. (For discussion of poetic terminology see Watson pages 11-15 and 160-200.)

It should be pointed out that mere segmentation of the poem into strophes and stanzas or from half-lines to stanzas tells us little about the relations of these component parts, and in particular how the various poetic features such as imagery, parallelism, meter, acrostics, and personification are worked into the poem and how rhetorical features are played out within this poem and other texts outside the poem. However, before we can consider poetic relatedness, we must complete the structural picture and explain its basis.

In strict anatomical terms we may say that Lamentations 1 consists of 134 half-lines, 67 lines, 22 verses, 9 strophes, and 2 stanzas. This counting of the parts is not particularly instructive. It would be somewhat more helpful to know, for example, the basis for the grouping of verses into strophes and of strophes into stanzas. The following display shows this segmentation. The numbers under "Lines" and "Half-lines" is the total of these in each strophe. The number of half-lines is always double the number of lines. Verse 7 is bracketed to show that it is exceptional and does not fit the criterion required for belonging to stanza II.

		Strophes	Verses	Lines	Half-lines
Poem	Stanza I	1.	1-3	9	18
		2.	4-6	9	18
		3.	7-9	10	20
		4.	10-11	6	12
	Stanza II	5.	12-14	9	18
		6.	15-16	6	12
		{?	17	3	6}
		7.	18-20	9	18
		8.	21-22	6	12

Strophe and stanza segmentation

It is quite clear that this poem has twenty-two verses and each verse is marked by one of the twenty-two letters of the Hebrew alphabet. Therefore the entire poem is delineated by the alphabet, and the next poem begins and ends with the same letters. There is accordingly a clear structural break between the poems (chapters). However, the arrangement of strophes and stanzas is not obvious and needs therefore to be explained. It must be stated that the segmentation of verses into strophes as given here is not the only one possible and may appear at times to be somewhat arbitrary.

Strophe 1 (verses 1-3): The feature of contrast is exhibited here, in which the former glory of Jerusalem is contrasted with its present humiliation. The city's present humiliations in verses 1 and 2 leads to the consequences in verse 3. Formerly full of people, now lonely; formerly great among the nations, now like a widow; formerly a princess, now a vassal; formerly a lover, now no one to comfort her; formerly her friends, now her enemies. Verse 3: exile, suffering, servitude, and distress.

Strophe 2 (verses 4-6): Although verses 3 and 4 display a series of consequences, there is a break between them in that verse 4 shifts to more specific aspects of "the city," particularly of the temple: the roads to Zion, her gates, her priests, her maidens. The contrast of past with present is here implied by presenting only the present suffering and humiliation. In the first strophe humiliation led to suffering. At the center of the second strophe we find the cause of Jerusalem's suffering. Verse 6 returns again to the feature of contrast: daughter of Zion, majesty departed; princes, like harts.

Strophe 3 (verses 7-9): Verse 7 forms a break with the preceding verses by naming "the city" for the first time. The past-present contrast is continued in only one line. Verse 8 binds with verse 7 by repeating Jerusalem. The opening of verse 8 expresses the cause of the events in verses 7 and 8. Verse 9 joins verse 8 by repeating the theme of sinfulness by using the image of menstruation and uncleanliness. Verse 9 breaks with what follows by closing with the first of several refrain-like pleas addressed to the LORD.

Strophe 4 (verses 10-11): Although verse 9 closes with reference to the enemy, and verse 10 opens with a similar expression, verse 10 introduces for the first time the pronouns "you" and "your," referring to the LORD. Verse 11 makes specific the sufferings of the people and then again closes with another plea addressed to the LORD.

Strophe 5 (verses 12-14): For the first time the poet addresses the reader or listener with "you plural" in Hebrew. Verses 13 and 14 specify the suffering the reader is told to look at in verse 12. These are the punishments given by the LORD.

Strophe 6 (verses 15-16): In these verses the speaker continues to be Jerusalem. Verse 16 gives the consequences of the LORD's action in verse 15.

Verse 17: The speaker is the poet and not Jerusalem. In this way verse 17 is similar to verses 1-11 and different from verses 12-22. This verse may be considered a strophe of its own, or a strophe belonging to those from 1 to 4. We may also consider it a purposeful break in the second stanza.

Strophe 7 (verses 18-20): These two verses are a continuous confession expressed by Jerusalem speaking in the first person.

Strophe 8 (verses 21-22): These final verses share a plea addressed to the LORD that Jerusalem's enemies should suffer as she has suffered.

The largest segmentation of Lamentations 1 is here called a stanza. The first is made up of strophes 1-4 (verses 1-11), in which the poet speaks of Jerusalem, using the third person singular pronouns "she" and "her." In the final half-line of verse 11, the poet switches to the first person singular "I" and "me." The first person is used in strophes 5, 6, 7, and 8 (verses 12-16 and verses 18-22). Verse 17 is exceptional. The two stanzas, which are unbalanced due to verse 17, together make up the poem. See the display above.

Special poetic features

There are several poetic features that are at the heart of nearly every line of Lamentations and need to be discussed in a general way at this point.

Parallelism

A feature of line arrangement is a tendency for adjoining half-lines to be ordered by matching elements of meaning or structure. Parallelism is a form of repetition with a deliberate rhetorical effect and plays an important role in biblical poetry, particularly in regard to rhetorical function. For a detailed statement of parallelism, see *A Handbook on Psalms* and *A Handbook on the Book of Job.*

Alphabetic acrostics

Each chapter of Lamentations has twenty-two verses, except chapter 3, which has sixty-six verses arranged in twenty-two groups of three. The arrangement into twenty-two verses or groups of verses in chapters 1-4 is to accommodate the verses to the twenty-two letters of the Hebrew alphabet. In chapters 1, 2, and 4 the first word in each verse begins with the successive letter of the Hebrew alphabet. That is, the first word in 1.1 begins with *alef,* the first word in 1.2 with *beth,* the first word in 1.3 with *gimel,* and so forth through the twenty-two letters of the alphabet.

Much has been said concerning the purpose of beginning each new line or verse with the next letter of the Hebrew alphabet. It is no doubt true that acrostics served to assist the ancients in memorizing the text. Acrostics may also have served the rhetorical function of creating the feeling that the poem was whole or complete. It was, after all, a poem that covered everything "from A to Z." Acrostics are uncommon enough to lend a feeling of novelty to a poem, and as such may give the poem a greater impact. This device when accompanied by a fixed metrical rhythm was doubtless a challenge to the skills of the poet, but it had the effect of relating the acrostic poem to other such poems in the Old Testament and thus gave the reader a feeling of being on familiar ground.

Meter

Meter in Hebrew poetry is often discussed as if the number of stresses or accents in a line is clear and easily determined. This is far from reflecting the linguistic facts. The main problem is that scholars do not know, and have no means of knowing, exactly how biblical poetry sounded when it was written. The indications of accent and vocalization in the Hebrew Bible were written down more than a thousand years after the poems themselves. It is necessary, therefore, to accept what is said about meter with a good deal of caution.

The rhythmic beat most commonly found in biblical poetry is the 3 + 3 meter. This is to be interpreted as three beats in a thought unit followed by the same number of beats in the next thought unit. Such a metric pattern creates a balanced line. The pattern that has been observed in Lamentations and in other Old Testament laments is unbalanced. There the typical rhythmic pattern is three beats in the first half-line followed by two beats in the second half-line. The name given to this unbalanced pattern is *qinah,* the Hebrew word for "lament." Although the *qinah* metrical pattern is common, particularly in chapters 1, 2, and 4 of Lamentations, there is a variety of other patterns as well. It is also the case that not all laments in the Old Testament are written in the *qinah* style, and furthermore this pattern is also found outside of the lament genre.

Meter determines the tempo or speed at which the poem is to be read or recited. The *qinah* meter is said to be a slow, measured rhythm fitting for a dirge.

Before turning to the detailed discussion of the poem, it is important to call attention to the rhetorical functions which these structural features serve. We must bear in mind that chapter 1 of Lamentations expresses the horror and grief caused by the defeat of Jerusalem and the destruction of the Temple. The reader listens to a weeping voice in which tears, cries, groans, the sounds of agony and anguish wash over him like waves. The repetitious nature of the structures discussed above reinforces the slow cyclical movement of the poem. Just as there is no escape from the affliction that has struck Jerusalem, neither is there much relief from the restrictive forms of the poem. This compatibility between form and function gives the poem a remarkable sense of unity and coherence.

A further rhetorical effect of these structural features is to create a powerful linkage with other laments in the Old Testament.

Comments on the poem

There follows now a verse-by-verse discussion of Lamentations chapter 1. In the first stanza (verses 1-11) the poet writes of the pitiful conditions of the city of Jerusalem by contrasting its destruction with its past glories. In the second stanza (verses 12-22) the point of view changes, and Jerusalem speaks of herself in the first person, except in verse 17, where there is a switch back to the third person. The RSV text is used to present the Hebrew form unless stated otherwise.

The major poetic device employed by the poet is the humanizing of Jerusalem. By causing an inanimate object to think, feel, and even to speak as human beings do (in particular a woman and mother), the poet enables the reader to identify with the humiliation and suffering of the people of Jerusalem.

1.1

As was pointed out earlier, each verse of chapter 1 has three lines, except verse 7, which has four. Verse 1 is particularly important as the opening because of its formal structure. There are three aspects of this structure that require comment. The first is the fact that the three lines are time-contrasting parallels. This means that in the first two lines the present condition of the city is given in the first half-line and the contrasting bygone greatness is given in the second half-line. In the third line this order is reversed. The second poetic feature is that the first two lines are linked by the repetition of *rabbati,* while the third unit is again linked in sound to the first two by the similar sounding *sharati.* Furthermore the second and third lines are in the form of a chiasmus:

A: How like a widow she has become
  B: She that was great among the nations
  B′: She that was a princess among the cities
A′: (She) has become a vassal

How lonely sits the city that was full of people! How opens the first line of the poem and is repeated in the next line as well as in 2.1 and 4.1. **How** not only provides the Hebrew title of the book but also gives unity to the opening of these three chapters. The Hebrew form of this word *'eykah* is the longer and more poetic form of *'eyk* used more commonly in prose writing. The opening of Lamentations links up clearly with the elegy in Isaiah 1.21, "How the faithful city has become a harlot." There are intertextual linkages to similar statements in Jeremiah 9.18; 48.17. In these passages **How** is not only exclamatory, it also depicts a change usually from virtue to vice, from past greatness to present shame. The shorter form may also be used in a similar way; for example, Ecclesiastes 2.16 "How the wise man dies just like the fool!"

How lonely hints that the city is being personified. The word rendered **lonely** suggests a state of isolation or solitariness, and in this context abandonment by the people who once lived there. This sense is confirmed by the second half-line **that was full of people**. However, there is also the possible meaning that the destruction of the temple has caused the LORD to abandon Zion, and thus the city is **lonely**. **Sits** agrees grammatically with the feminine gender of **city**. In this way the Hebrew reader is prepared for the association of **city** with the female images that follow.

We may ask how within the text of the poem the original readers would understand **city** to refer to Jerusalem, a fact that is not disclosed fully until verse 7. One answer is that verses 1 through 6 are replete with replacement expressions that convey the sense of Jerusalem. In verse 1, for example, **full of people, great among the nations, princess among the cities.** In verse 3 she is associated with **Judah**, in verse 4 with **Zion,** and in verse 6 with **daughter of Zion.** GNB overrides this poetic progression by naming Jerusalem in verse 1. See also verse 11.

In the Hebrew poem the rhetorical progression from **city** to **Jerusalem** is a poetic movement that takes the reader through a well-planned series of personifications. In verse 1 she is reduced from being **great** to being a **widow**, from **princess** to **slave**. In verse 2 she **weeps** and is without **comfort**. This gradual unfolding of her humiliation as described in verses 1-6 is depicted in humanizing analogies that serve to draw the reader into the tragedy that is this city and its people.

That was full of people contrasts with the sense of the first half-line and speaks of her former times, just as the second parallelism does.

How like a widow: How functions the same as in the first line and has the rhetorical function of emphasizing what was said in the first line. **Like a widow** shifts to a simile, a device that invites the reader to compare the abandoned city to a woman who mourns for her dead husband. The comparison may be to Jerusalem's isolation from other cities, but more likely **like a widow** suggests that the LORD has departed (but is not dead) and left the city without protection and support.

Great among the nations: the poet uses hyperbole or exaggeration in speaking of Jerusalem as great or greatest among the nations.

She that was a princess: this half-line is parallel in sense to the second half-line of the previous line. Here again the female figure (queen, noble lady) represents the city.

Has become a vassal: the word rendered **vassal** refers to a person forced into labor for a conqueror. The image of the city as a female slave brings the progressive humiliation to a peak. The poet avoids the use of the simile, which he used in **like a widow,** and expresses the image through a direct metaphor, which strengthens the impact of the series of figures used in the first three lines of verse 1.

1.2

She weeps bitterly in the night: in verse 1 the poet established the contrast between past glory and present dishonor. In verse 2 he sets out to describe the city's humiliation in terms of what she does. The first of these events is her weeping. The poet thus begins with the sounds made by the agonizing widow. These are sounds heard **in the night**, the time when other sounds are hushed.

Tears on her cheeks shifts from the voice of her weeping to the feeling of hot tears on her face. Jerusalem will again be depicted in verse 16 as weeping and with tears flowing from her eyes.

Among all her lovers introduces a new thought into the poem, one that raises the question of her guilt. Her **lovers** are many and so suggests that her infidelities have been many. This half-line strikes a common chord with Psalm 88, which opens with a similar thought, "I cry out in the night before thee," and goes on to say in verse 18 "Thou has caused lover and friend to shun me." In this way the poet links his thought to a common theme of Israel's faithless allies. This is also seen in the metaphors of Hosea, Jeremiah, and Ezekiel, in which Israel, the wife of Yahweh, has been unfaithful by entering into alliances with foreign nations and their gods.

She has none to comfort her: in Hebrew this half-line precedes **among all her lovers.** The poet's thought is linked back to verse 2 and forward to verses 3, 9, 16, 17, and 21. The consequence is that Jerusalem's lack of comforters is firmly foregrounded in chapter 1.

All her friends have dealt treacherously with her: the third line exhibits intensification. Not only do **her friends** (a matching term for **lovers)** fail to comfort her, her friends deal deceitfully with her and become her enemies. The thought and language of this parallelism is again linked with verses 3, 5, 7, 9, 10, 19, and 21.

1.3

Judah has gone into exile because of affliction: it is unlikely that the Hebrew can be translated **because of affliction**. The statement describes Judah's present condition, not its cause. GNB is better, with "Judah's people are helpless slaves." The poet mentions the kingdom of Judah by name. This is poetically significant because he reserves the personification for the city of Jerusalem. By mentioning Judah the poet has broadened the geographical and political perspective of the poem to make the suffering more inclusive. In 2.1 he will speak of the "splendor of Israel," "the habitation of Jacob," and "the daughter of Judah." However in chapter 1, aside from the first line of verse 3, the focus rests unwaveringly upon personified Jerusalem.

The word rendered **affliction** is one of a skein of terms which shares a common semantic area in chapter 1 and gives the poem an unfragmented unity of thought.

She dwells now among the nations: dwells, which translates the same verb rendered **sits** in verse 1, recalls the isolation of the lonely and humiliated city. **Nations** here refers to foreign nations or foreign peoples.

But finds no resting place: Judah's people are forced to live in captivity among foreigners. **Resting place** stands in sharp contrast with **dwell among the nations**. In Deuteronomy 12.9 the conquest of the land, the inheritance from the LORD, was to provide a resting place, a place to live safely and securely from the threat of enemies.

Her pursuers have all overtaken her: pursuers translates one of three Hebrew synonyms used in chapter 1. The dramatic picture painted by the poet is not clearly revealed in RSV. **In the midst of her distress** is probably a reference to a military pursuit in which a fleeing army is driven into a narrow pass where it can be ambushed. GNB renders it "Surrounded by enemies with no way to escape."

1.4

Verse 4 expands the image of Jerusalem's agony by fixing our attention on the loss of worship in the temple. In this verse the poet personifies **roads** and **gates**, which are then followed by two human subjects, **priests** and **maidens**. **The roads to Zion mourn**: these are the roads to the temple which would be crowded with worshippers on festival days. This line echoes verse 1, in which the city is depicted as a widow in mourning. There the city was once full of people and now is forsaken by the people who once worshiped. The figure of the mourning roads returns in verse 20, where "in the street the sword bereaves."

All her gates are desolate: in the second line **gates** are personified as being **desolate**. It is not certain whether these are the gates of the city or the gates of the temple. However, in the context of **Zion**, **priests**, and **maidens**, the reference is probably to the gates or entrances to the temple. **Desolate** reinforces the thoughts expressed by such terms as "lonely," "none to comfort," "none come." These gates are in rhetorical contrast to the use of gates in "gates of the daughter of Zion" (Psa 9.14), "Lift up your heads, O gates" (Psa 24.7), "Enter his gates with thanksgiving" (Psa 100.4).

Her priests groan resonates with Joel 1.9, "The priests mourn." Their groaning is brought on by the destruction of the temple. **Her maidens have been dragged away**: the Hebrew text has "afflicted." The reference to **maidens** (literally "virgins") is not young women in general but in the context of the temple refers to young women who took part in the celebrations on festival days.

She herself suffers bitterly: again the poet returns to speak of Jerusalem as the suffering woman.

The image of mourning in verse 4 forms an intertextual link with such passages as Joel 1.10, in which "The fields are laid waste, the ground mourns"; Hosea 4.3 "The land mourns, and all who dwell in it languish." In the Joel reference the wine and oil fail, in Hosea the beasts of the field, the birds of the air, and the fish of the sea are taken away. In our poem it is the maidens who are dragged away.

1.5

In verse 5 the first line proclaims the success of Jerusalem's enemies. The second gives the reason for their victory, and the third relates one of the consequences of Jerusalem's demise. Jerusalem is referred to by "her" five times in this verse. RSV's rendering **Her foes have become the head** would be better translated, for example, "Her enemies have become her masters." However, the poet has a purpose in using the word **head** as he is turning the reader's thought to Deuteronomy 28, which lays out the consequence of Israel's disobedience. After saying that disobedience will take Israel into captivity, verse 44 adds "He (the enemy) shall lend to you, and you shall not lend to him; he shall be the head, and you shall be the tail."

Two of the three words used in chapter 1 referring to enemies are found in parallel in the two half-lines of the first line of verse 5. **Her enemies prosper** is literally "Her enemies are at ease," which probably means that the Babylonians won an easy victory in the siege of Jerusalem, particularly because the LORD gave it to them. **Because the LORD has made her suffer:** the poet does not attribute Babylonia's victory to their superior arms or masterful military strategy. Rather it is the LORD who has caused Jerusalem to fall. This theme is intensified in the second half of the poem, also in 2.16, and particularly in 3.1b-18. Outside of Lamentations the warning of punishment associated with disobedience to the covenant is particularly marked in Deuteronomy 28 and Leviticus 26. Consequently the poem forms a powerful link with this teaching in the Pentateuch.

For the multitude of her transgressions: the word rendered **transgressions** makes explicit the nature of the wrong Israel has committed and so brought on her downfall. The term refers to rebellion against the LORD but also has here a political nuance. For example, the verb is used in 2 Kings 1.1; 3.5 to refer to Moab's rebellion against the king of Israel. The poetic progression in verse 5 moves from an allusion to the covenant in the first unit to sin (rebellion against the covenant) in the second, and then to the consequence of these acts in the third.

Her children . . . captives before the foe: the final unit returns to the personification of Jerusalem as a mother. The image of children forced to separate from their mother is a powerful figure and is intended to strike the reader's deeper emotions.

1.6

The first two lines of verse 6 again speak of conditions and persons who no longer exist. In this part of the verse the poet returns to the present shame as contrasted with the past honor. These were dealt with explicitly in verse 1. **From the daughter of Zion . . . :** here the poet expands the humanizing of Jerusalem. In so doing he links his language to such passages as Isaiah 1.8; 10.32; Jeremiah 4.31. He will again extend this expression to create the parallel form "daughter of Judah" in verse 15 and "daughter of my people" in 2.11. It is possible that the connection between verses 5 and 6 was made so that the reader would understand that the loss of Jerusalem's children is the **majesty** that has departed. If this is not so, **majesty** refers to the pomp, honor, glory, beauty of former times.

Her princes have become like harts: princes refers not to the sons of kings but more generally to leaders or rulers. **Like harts** is the second simile the poet has introduced among many metaphors. The first was "like a widow" in verse 1. **Harts,** which refer to male deer or stags, translates a word that could be interpreted as "stag" or "ram." In the context of the hunter, stag is preferred. In his usage of **princes like harts,** the poet has reversed the usual transfer of nonanimate to human and builds the figure from the human to the nonhuman. The switch in imaging not only gives greater variety to the poem, but it also opens a new perspective for understanding still another aspect of the humiliation of the people of Jerusalem. The hunter image will occur again in 3.5.

In the final half-line of this verse, **before the pursuer** matches the final half-line of verse 5, **before the foe**. In verse 5 it is the children captured by the foe, and in verse 6 the rulers hunted down by the hunter.

1.7

Verse 7 is exceptional in that the Hebrew text has four lines, that is, eight half-lines instead of the usual six. It is uncertain why at this point a change is made in the number of lines. The established pattern of three lines to a verse is unexpectedly broken. **Jerusalem remembers** shifts from the active things she does to her mental reflections. What she remembers are **all the precious things that were hers from days of old**. These things are not specified, but the line is similar to "all her majesty" in the first unit of verse 6.

There was none to help her repeats the theme of "she has none to comfort her" in verse 2, and is found again in verses 9, 16, 17, and 21.

The foe gloated over her: gloated translates a verb meaning "to see," and in this context it is a special kind of seeing or staring with evil satisfaction derived from Jerusalem's humiliation. The thought is linked to many similar passages in the Old Testament, and the poet returns to it in 3.14, "I have become the laughingstock of all peoples." Outside of Lamentations it is found, for example, in Psalm 37.13; 52.6; Proverbs 1.26; Job 30.1.

Mocking at her downfall parallels in meaning the preceding half-line of this final line.

1.8

Jerusalem sinned grievously: the personification continues as this line picks up the thought expressed in the second line of verse 5. The second half-line says literally "For that reason she has become *nidah,*" a word which occurs only here. Some interpreters take *nidah* to refer to an object of scorn and so translate "People shake their heads at her." RSV and others make a slight change in the word to get **filthy** or "unclean." In this case the reference is to the ceremonial uncleanliness of a woman during menstruation, as explained in Leviticus 12.2, 5; 15.19-24. If this thought is correct, it links verse 8 to verse 9.

For they have seen her nakedness: this statement links up with that expressed in Ezekiel 16.37, where Jerusalem is represented as a woman stripped naked in the sight of her "lovers." The image of **nakedness** is disgrace, and stripping off the clothing was a punishment for an adulterous woman, as in Hosea 2.3. The expression is used metaphorically of the punishment of nations in 4.21; Isaiah 47.2-3; and in Nahum 3.5.

Verse 8 ends with semantic parallelism in which **she groans** from the shame of her humiliation, and in the second half-line her groan is converted to action as **she turns her face away** to hide her shame.

1.9

In verse 9 the poet intensifies the image of the disgraced naked female. **Her uncleanliness was in her skirts:** if **filthy** in verse 8 refers to her menstrual blood, then that blood is now seen as staining her clothing. **She took no thought of her doom:** Isaiah 47.7 uses similar language with regard to Babylon depicted as a woman. **She has no comforter** echoes the words from the second line of verses 2 and 7.

"O LORD, behold my affliction . . . triumphed!" RSV treats this as a prayer uttered by the personified Jerusalem. If we accept these as the words of Jerusalem, the poet has carried poetic personification to its peak in that the city now speaks, even pleads. GNB leaves no doubt about the speaker when it translates in verse 11 " 'Look at me, LORD,' the city cries; 'see me in my misery.' " This quotation may be taken as anticipating the shift in viewpoint to the first person, which takes place starting with the final line of verse 11.

1.10

In verse 10 our attention is drawn to the temple that has been destroyed by the invaders. **The enemy has stretched out his hands over all her precious things:** the poet uses a figurative expression **stretch out hands over** to mean rob, plunder, carry off. What the enemy has plundered is the temple treasures. These events are described in 2 Kings 25.13-17.

In verse 7 the poet spoke of "all the precious things." There the reference was general, but in verse 10 the same expression is applied to the wealth of the temple.

She has seen the nations invade her sanctuary: she again represents Jerusalem and refers to what the people of the city have witnessed. **Nations** translates the Hebrew *goyim* and refers to all non-Israelites, and in this case specifically to the invading Babylonians. This is the first explicit mention of the temple, although indirect references have been made in the first two lines of verse 4.

Those whom thou didst forbid to enter thy congregation: here the poet links his statement to Deuteronomy 23.3, where particular nations are mentioned: "No Ammonite or Moabite shall enter the assembly of the LORD; even to the tenth generation . . . ." Although there is no evidence that Ammonites or Moabites took part in the destruction of Jerusalem on this historic occasion, it appears the poet has taken the liberty to extend the command to all the *goyim*.

There is no doubt a degree of irony in the thought that no heathen was to enter the temple no matter how peaceful and religious his intentions. The Babylonians who entered did so with the express purpose of plundering and destroying it.

1.11

In verse 11, which is the final verse of the first stanza of chapter 1, the only use of personification is **her people**. The poet describes the pathos of the people struggling to prevent starvation. **All her people groan as they search for bread:** it should be noticed that the poet uses **groan** as a response to deprivation. For example, in verse 4 the priests groan because of the loss of the temple. In verse 8 Jerusalem groans because her clothing is taken away. In verse 11 the people groan for lack of food.

They trade their treasures for food: treasures translates the same word used in verses 7 and 10, "precious things." These may refer to valuable personal possessions. However, if the poet is depicting the pathos of starvation among a people who have been robbed and plundered, it is more likely that the word is used as in Hosea 9.16, referring to their small children. In 2.20 mothers are driven to eat their own offspring. In this case the poet creates a valued inanimate figure to represent human beings.

The third line of verse 11 closes the first stanza of the poem with a cry addressed to the LORD. **Look, O LORD, and behold**, a close formal rendering of the Hebrew, "See, Yahweh, and look," in which two verbs of similar meaning serve to strengthen the plea. This plea serves as a closing refrain for strophes 3 and 4.

In verses 12-22 Jerusalem speaks in the first person (except in verse 17). The use of first person serves to intensify the personification of the city. In this way we see a major break in the poem, in which the second stanza displays a shift to greater emotional impact and deeper involvement for the reader/listener.

1.12

The first half-line of verse 12 is unclear in Hebrew. However, it appears that Jerusalem, the speaker, is calling out to anyone who may not be involved in her tragedy to stop and see for themselves if anyone has suffered the way she has. **Which the LORD inflicted:** this thought, introduced first in verse 5, is now repeated and becomes progressively developed in the second half of chapter 1. **On the day of his fierce anger:** the reference here is normally to the "Day of the LORD," an event which the prophets expected to take place in the future, as in Amos 5.18-20. However, there is here a switch in expectations, because that **day** has already come. Instead of it being a day in which the LORD wins a victory over Israel's enemies, it turns out to be a day in which the LORD uses Israel's enemies to crush her.

1.13

The poet now creates a series of metaphors to describe the way in which the LORD dealt with Jerusalem. **From on high he sent fire**: at one level the reader is reminded of the destruction of Sodom and Gomorrah in Genesis 19. On the other hand the fire is sent **into my bones,** in which case the reference may be to a burning fever. The Hebrew text has "From on high he sent fire into my bones. He is the master of it," which has never been clearly explained.

The second metaphor is **he spread a net for my feet.** This image links up with many Old Testament passages such as Jeremiah 50.24; Ezekiel 12.13; 17.20; 32.3; Hosea 7.12; Psalm 94.13. This is followed by **He turned me back,** referring to being unable to walk along a path because the LORD blocks the way.

In the final line the LORD has abandoned Jerusalem and left her **stunned** in the first half-line and **faint** or sick in the second.

1.14

The Hebrew text of verse 14 is uncertain, and HOTTP mentions five places where the text is in dispute. However, if we follow the HOTTP recommendations, we are fairly close to RSV. **My transgressions were bound into a yoke; by his hand they were fastened together:** the image of fashioning a yoke from the people's sins is a powerful metaphor of guilt and punishment for people acquainted with the function of the yoke on draft animals. The **yoke** of sins is placed upon the neck of Jerusalem, and she is subjected to and controlled by the enemy who drives her.

The final line adds no extension to the yoke figure but says that the LORD has placed Jerusalem in this humiliating position.

1.15

In verse 15 Jerusalem speaks about the fate of her people. These are **my mighty men,** which probably refers to her soldiers, **my young men** who are those strong and able, the future of Israel, **the virgin daughter of Judah,** meaning the people of Judah. In the first line the LORD has rejected the efforts of Jerusalem's defenders. In the second line the LORD **summoned an assembly against me.** This **assembly** is not a body of citizens of Jerusalem but a metaphorical way of saying "He called upon a foreign army, whose orders were to crush the defenders of the city."

In the third line the poet introduces the image of the winepress, a figure of the LORD punishing his people. This line is parallel to that used in Isaiah 63.1-6. In verse 3 the poet spoke of Judah, and here he refers to

the virgin daughter of Judah, yet another form of the personification of Jerusalem.

1.16

For these things I weep; my eyes flow with tears: the first line of verse 16 displays typical poetic parallelism, in which **weep** is matched by the more enlivened image **eyes flow with tears**. The second half-line recalls the image of the second half-line in verse 2. It is uncertain why the Hebrew text has "my eye my eye," although some interpreters think it is a way of speaking of both eyes.

A comforter is far from me is a manner of saying that Jerusalem is without anyone to comfort her, a thought that is repeated from verses 2 and 9 and is thus emphasized. **Comforter** is matched in the next half-line by **one to revive my courage.**

My children may refer to the inhabitants of Jerusalem, but more likely, with Jerusalem personified as a mother, these are the young ones of the city, a repetition of the thought in verse 11.

1.17

In verse 17 the poet ceases to use the first person and reverts to the third person. There is a clear shift of emphasis in that the poet speaks about Zion instead of Zion speaking for herself. Therefore verse 17 interrupts the point of view held otherwise throughout the second stanza. In this verse it is set forth that the LORD is the one who has ordered the events that led to the downfall of Jerusalem, a theme that began in verse 5.

Zion stretches out her hands: in verse 10 the same verb followed by "over" carried the sense of rob or plunder. Here the thought is that she puts out her hands asking for aid and comfort, which is made clear by the following half-line, **but there is none to comfort her**, a thought that links back to verses 2, 9, and 16.

In the second line of this verse, the poet introduces yet another name for the personified city, **Jacob**. If **Jacob** is being used to represent all of Israel, the poet is here widening the perspective in a similar manner as he did in the use of Judah in verse 3.

The LORD has commanded against Jacob that his neighbors should be his foes: in this line the use of the masculine **Jacob** forces the poet to drop the image of the female figure, although only momentarily. It is the LORD who calls those who live around **Jacob** to become his enemies and attack him.

Jerusalem has become a filthy thing: filthy thing translates the same Hebrew word used in verse 8. The repetition serves to foreground the idea that Jerusalem is defiled or tabooed like a menstruating woman, and as a consequence she is isolated.

1.18

Verse 18 clearly marks a break with verse 17, as from verse 18 to the end of the chapter Jerusalem again speaks in the first person. The first line of verse 18 begins as a confession that continues through verse 20. **The LORD is in the right**: the speaker confesses that the LORD has done right to cause the downfall of Jerusalem. The language employed here is drawn from legal usage. The complete expression may be seen in Exodus 9.27, in which Pharaoh says to Moses and Aaron "The LORD is in the right, and I and my people are in the wrong."

Rebelled against his word: in Hebrew the rebellion is said to be against "his mouth." The poet is using synecdoche, or "a part for the whole," in which "his mouth" represents the LORD and his commands, his laws. The second unit of the confession is a warning addressed not just to Israel but to everyone. They are warned to look at the suffering of Jerusalem, which is here **My maidens and my young men have gone into captivity**. These groups have been mentioned in verses 4 and 15 as being taken captive or crushed by the enemy.

1.19

The confession continues in verse 19. **I called to my lovers:** here Jerusalem admits openly that she failed to trust the LORD. The poet picks up the image of **lovers** as used in verse 2 to refer to her political allies. In verse 2 these persons dealt treacherously with her. In the confession their treatment is more terse: **they deceived me.**

In the second and third lines of this verse, the confession gives way to what appears to be an appeal for sympathy, which actually began in verse 18. **My priests and elders perished in the city**. The poet concluded verse 18 speaking of the deportation of her young men and women. In verse 19 we encounter the authorities and older people who died in the city from starvation. The two pictures serve rhetorically to give a sense of completeness to this tale of woe.

1.20

The cry for sympathy continues. The first line offers a parallelism of striking effect. Jerusalem cries out **"I am in distress,"** which is matched in the second half-line by a vivid image, which is literally "My intestines are in ferment." Here the poet carries the idea of **distress** to a higher pitch through the use of a metaphor in the second half-line.

In the second line the poet offers another anatomical image to refer to the emotions, which is literally "My heart is turned over within me." The reason for the emotional state is then given as **because I have been very rebellious**, in which **rebellious** is derived from the same root as used in verse 18. With this the confession is essentially completed.

In verse 19 the priests and elders perish in their search for food. In verse 20 death is again the topic, but now it is expressed as **In the street the sword bereaves**. The poet speaks of two places: **in the street**, which is literally "outdoors," and **in the house**. The two expressions serve to give the sense of "everywhere."

The sword bereaves is a further example of the poet's inclination to humanize inanimate objects. The sword which kills deprives the survivors of their loved ones. It is difficult to be certain whom the sword slays. It may be anyone or the reference may be to her children. GNB avoids saying who is killed, by translating "There is murder in the streets." The poet concludes the third line with a simile, **in the house it is like death**. It is clear that **bereaves** is matched by **death**, but it is not so evident what is referred to as being **like death**. Many suggestions have been made, and some interpreters change the text to get "famine." Others take it to refer to the plague or to Sheol, as in Psalm 6.5.

1.21

Again the city appeals for sympathy: **Hear how I groan**. This is the fourth time someone is said to groan, and the fifth time there is no one to **comfort her**. The groans here are echoed by more groans at the end of verse 22. In this way the final two verses form a single strophe. The second line shifts attention to Jerusalem's enemies, who have heard of her misfortune. Even these enemies know and are glad that the LORD has made her suffer.

If we accept the third line as an imperative, Jerusalem is asking the LORD to curse or punish her enemies. In 1.12 **the day** refers to the time when God judged and punished Israel. However, here that expression refers to the coming judgment of the LORD against Israel's enemies. The plea is that the LORD make her enemies suffer as she is suffering.

1.22

Verse 22 concludes chapter 1 and expands verse 21 in the first line: **Let all their evil doing come before thee; and deal with them.** The first half-line is idiomatic and means "Punish them for their wicked deeds." The speaker desires swift retribution from the LORD. We may render the second half-line "Treat them as you have treated me." **Because of all my transgressions** picks up the language and thought from verse 5.

Chapter 1 of Lamentations ends with **For my groans are many**: this expression forms a close parallel with the final half-line, **and my heart is faint**, an expression that strikes a familiar rhetorical chord with such passages as Psalm 40.12; 61.2; Job 19.27; 23.16.

Conclusion

Most commentaries on Lamentations fail to consider structural arrangements above the verse level. This article has attempted to show how a chapter of Lamentations may be viewed both below and above the verse division. Furthermore, the verse-by-verse comments have been given with particular emphasis upon the poetic features in the text. It would be instructive to follow these up to see the various ways the poem's structural features lend themselves to liturgical arrangement of the poem. However, that is a task beyond the scope of this article.

References

Versions cited

Good News Bible: The Bible in Today's English Version. 1976, 1979. New York: American Bible Society. (Cited as GNB.)

The Holy Bible: Revised Standard Version. 1952, 1971, 1973. New York: Division of Christian Education of the National Council of the Churches of Christ in the United States of America. (Cited as RSV.)

UBS Translators' Handbooks

Bratcher, R.G., and W.D. Reyburn. 1991. *A Handbook on Psalms.* New York: United Bible Societies.

Reyburn, W.D. 1992. *A Handbook on the Book of Job.* New York: United Bible Societies.

———. 1992. *A Handbook on Lamentations.* New York: United Bible Societies.

Commentaries and other works

Gordis, Robert. 1954, 1968, 1974. *The Song of Songs and Lamentations: A Study, Modern Translation, and Commentary.* Revised and Augmented Edition. New York: KTAV Publishing House.

Gottwald Norman K. 1985. *The Hebrew Bible: A Socio-literary Introduction.* Philadelphia: Fortress Press.

Hillers, Delbert R. 1972. *Lamentations: Introduction, Translation, and Notes* (The Anchor Bible). New York: Doubleday.

Kugel, James L. 1981 *The Idea of Biblical Poetry: Parallelism and Its History.* New Haven: Yale University Press.

Watson, W.G.E. 1984. *Classical Hebrew Poetry: A Guide to Its Techniques.* Journal for the Study of the Old Testament, Supplement Series 26. Sheffield, England.

Translating Moses' Song at the Sea

Noel D. Osborn

The story told in the Book of Exodus moves successively through four significant relationships, namely: Yahweh with Moses, Moses with Pharaoh, Moses with the People, and Yahweh with the People. The book therefore divides naturally into two parts at 15.22, following the crossing of the Red Sea, rather than with the Ten Commandments in chapter 20. The second part, of course, tells about the journey of the Israelites to Mount Sinai, where the Law was given and the Tabernacle built. But the first part shows how Yahweh delivered his people from slavery in Egypt before revealing to them the terms of this new covenant relationship. Theologically as well as structurally, therefore, Exodus clearly shows how God's grace precedes the people's obligation. This is what the Song at the Sea is all about.

The encounter with the king of Egypt had been brought to an end and the prolonged contest for freedom finally won with the miraculous deliverance at the sea. Moses' song in Exo 15.1-18, as well as Miriam's song in verse 21, provides a fitting climax to the period of Israel's slavery, and it introduces a change of direction and a new beginning for Israel as a nation.

This "Song at the Sea," is one of the finest examples of ancient Hebrew poetry in the Bible.[1] It uses archaic words and phrases that are powerful and descriptive, some of them reflecting ancient concepts about the creation of the universe out of chaos and confusion. The basic theme is the celebration of Yahweh's victory over Israel's greatest enemy and the establishment of a new nation of Yahweh's chosen people. The brief references to the deliverance at the sea and the journey to a new land are interspersed with outbursts of praise and thanksgiving to Yahweh. This hymn of praise was probably used in the public worship of the Israelite community from early times.

Translating this ancient song is especially difficult if one attempts to preserve the impact of the Hebrew poetic form and still be faithful to the intended meaning. This is because poetic form cannot readily be carried over from one language to another without some change in meaning or distortion of function. Figures of speech often need to be changed in order to convey the intended meaning. Inevitably something is lost, so it is usually necessary to compensate for this by introducing poetic features characteristic of the receptor language that will have the same or similar impact.

There are a number of features, such as rhyme, rhythm, and repetition, that give it a liturgical quality. The brief measured lines parallel one another and create an emotional tone conducive to worship. The meter is predominantly 2'2', with some occasional shifting to a 3'3' beat. Several key terms and ideas echo throughout the song, suggesting a parallelism of thought on a broader scale. The ambiguity of the time context, especially from verse 13 on, gives the song a timeless quality that has enabled Yahweh's people in all generations to relive this dramatic moment of deliverance.

Dividing the poem into strophes is somewhat subjective, for there are various clues that allow for different possibilities. Scholars have usually marked the divisions on the basis of the content rather than the numerous rhetorical features. For example, they call attention to the shift of theme in verse 13 from the deliverance at the sea to the wilderness wandering and the eventual entrance into the promised land. But the repeated outbursts of praise, in which Yahweh is addressed by name (verses 6, 11, and 16b-17), seem to function as responses to several brief accounts of what Yahweh did, and continues to do, in controlling the history of his chosen people.

Since the purpose of this article is simply to provide a verse-by-verse commentary relevant to translation, the rhetorical analysis of James Muilenburg is followed, with a few minor adaptations.[2] Muilenburg, sometimes referred to as "the father of rhetorical criticism," was more concerned with the formal features of the song as we now have it than with the unresolved questions of source-critical analysis. He consequently interpreted the song as a liturgy, dividing it into three parts, each of which includes a confession of faith, a brief narrative account, and a response of praise. His threefold pattern may be outlined as follows:

Introit (Call to Worship)	15.1b
I. Yahweh has defeated the Egyptians.	15.2-6
Confession	15.2-3
Narrative	15.4-5
Response	15.6
II. Yahweh is greater than all the gods.	15.7-11
Confession	15.7-8
Narrative	15.9-10
Response	15.11
III. Yahweh will establish his people.	15.12-17
Confession	15.12-13
Narrative	15.14-16a
Response	15.16b-17
Closing Doxology	15.18

In the discussion that follows, both RSV and GNB texts are given for each verse. RSV provides a basis for pointing out significant exegetical and rhetorical features. The significant discourse markers are noted as they occur. GNB, printed in italics, illustrates possible adjustments in translation. Although these adjustments often clarify the meaning, they sometimes do so at the expense of the poetic form. In the text and the commentary, words and phrases of RSV are in bold type, while those of GNB are in bold italics.[3]

The Introit

15.1 **Then Moses and the people of Israel sang this song to the LORD, saying,**

"I will sing to the LORD, for he has triumphed gloriously;
the horse and his rider he has thrown into the sea.

Then Moses and the Israelites sang this song to the LORD*:*
"I will sing to the LORD*, because he has won a glorious victory;*
he has thrown the horses and their riders into the sea.

The first part of the verse, of course, is the narrative introduction to the song, which begins at the second line. Note that **Moses and the people of Israel** (literally "the sons of Israel") are identified as the ones who **sang this song to the** LORD, that is, to Yahweh. There is no indication as to how this was sung, but probably **Moses** sang one or two lines and **the people** then responded with the same words. LORD, in capital letters, identifies the sacred name revealed to Moses at the burning bush (3.14-15). It appears ten times throughout the song, five times as a vocative ("O LORD"). The additional word, **saying**, may be omitted, since its function is simply to introduce the words of the song.

The first two lines of the song itself are like an introit, or call to worship. The same words are repeated in the Song of Miriam in verse 21. **I will sing to the** LORD may also be rendered as "I sing to the LORD," since the tense is not clearly indicated in the Hebrew. (See below at verse 13.) One may also say, "Let me sing to Yahweh." **For he has triumphed gloriously** is literally "being high he is high," or "he is very high." This idiom may be understood either as "he is highly exalted" (New American Standard Bible [NASB], Translator's Old Testament [TOT]) or as "he has risen up in triumph" (REB). Most translations prefer the second meaning, as in GNB: *he has won a glorious victory*.

The horse and his rider uses the singular to represent all *the horses and their riders*. The Hebrew uses the participle of the verb "to ride," but some read it as "chariot" (New American Bible [NAB], John I. Durham) by changing just one vowel. (See RSV footnote.) NJV has "horse and driver." **He has thrown into the sea** is a metaphor intended to emphasize Yahweh's swift action, so several translations (NJV, REB, NIV) use the more descriptive word "hurled." The Hebrew verb is found only here and in Jer 4.29, where it means to shoot an arrow.

I. Yahweh Has Defeated the Egyptians

15.2 **The** LORD **is my strength and my song,**
and he has become my salvation;

this is my God, and I will praise him,
my father's God, and I will exalt him.

The LORD *is my strong defender;*
he is the one who has saved me.
He is my God, and I will praise him,
my father's God, and I will sing about his greatness.

Verses 2-3 are a confession of faith. (See the threefold pattern above.) The first line has no verb, just three words that mean "my strength and my song Yah." Yah is a shortened form of the name Yahweh. **My strength** has been understood by some as "my fortress" or "my refuge" (REB), but the same word is used in verse 13, where "refuge" does not work. In some languages it may be easier to say, "The LORD gives me strength" or "makes me strong." The meaning of the word for **my song** is not certain. Some understand it to mean protection or defense. So GNB has: *The LORD is my strong defender.* **And he has become my salvation** is literally "and he is to me for help." In the setting of the Red Sea, this would mean *he is the one who has saved me.*

This is my God uses the word *'el,* a common word for "God" or "god" in several ancient cultures. **And I will praise him** is a word found only here, possibly meaning "to beautify." The Greek Septuagint has "I will glorify him" (REB). **My father's God**, literally "God of my father," means "the God my father worshiped" (see also 3.6). Here the more general term, *'elohim,* is used for **God**. **And I will exalt him** is literally "and I will make him high." GNB's *and I will sing about his greatness* brings out the meaning but destroys the balance with **"I will praise him.**"

15.3 **The LORD is a man of war; the LORD is his name.**

The LORD is a warrior; the LORD is his name.

The LORD is a man of war is literally "Yahweh a man of combat." Again there is no verb. If it is difficult to speak of Yahweh as a man, one may either say, *The LORD is a warrior,* or change the metaphor to simile, "Yahweh is like a man of war."

The LORD is his name is just two words, "Yahweh his name." The problem here is that the English word "Lord" is a title, not a name. It would be better to use "Yahweh" here, or at least have a footnote explaining that Yahweh is what is written, but *'adonay* ("Lord") is what is read aloud in Jewish tradition.

15.4 **"Pharaoh's chariots and his host he cast into the sea;**
and his picked officers are sunk in the Red Sea.

"He threw Egypt's army and its chariots into the sea;
the best of its officers were drowned in the Red Sea.

Verses 4-5 give a brief narrative account, but they are still poetic in form. The subject of the verb is Yahweh. **His host** refers to Pharaoh's "army" (NRSV). **He cast into the sea** means that Yahweh ***threw*** them into the sea. A different word is used in verse 1, but the meaning is the same. **His picked officers** means ***the best of his officers***. The word for **officers** means "third man," so it refers to the third man who rode in each chariot as the commander. The idea is that even ***the best*** men were drowned, including all the others as well. The word for ***drowned*** really means to be submerged, or sunk, whether it be in water or in mud (see Jer 38.6). **The Red Sea** follows the Greek Septuagint; the Hebrew is literally "Sea of Reeds." (See the commentaries for further explanation.)

15.5 **The floods cover them;**
they went down into the depths like a stone.

The deep sea covered them;
they sank to the bottom like a stone.

The floods is an ancient mythological term used for the primeval waters, or the watery chaos before the creation. The singular form, "the deep," is used in Gen 1.2. Here the plural is used, so "deep waters" (NIV) or ***deep sea*** is better. REB has "watery abyss." RSV translates this same word as "the deeps" in verse 8. **Cover them** is present tense in English, but others have ***covered them***. The tense is not indicated in the Hebrew, so one must interpret the context.

They went down is the usual word for descend, but here ***they sank*** seems appropriate. **Into the depths** is another word for the deep sea, so it is possible to say ***they sank to the bottom***. **Like a stone** is a simile that is repeated in different form in verses 10 and 16. As a discourse marker, it signals the end of the "narrative" and the beginning of the "response" in each of the three parts of the song. (See the threefold pattern above.)

15.6 **Thy right hand, O LORD, glorious in power,**
thy right hand, O LORD, shatters the enemy.

"Your right hand, LORD, is awesome in power;
it breaks the enemy in pieces.

This verse is the first of three responses. (See the threefold pattern above.) **Thy right hand** is the word referring to the right side rather than the left. Here in brief poetic form it refers to Yahweh's **right hand** as a symbol of his authority and **power**. **O LORD** is the first of several vocative uses of Yahweh where the poet addresses him by name. (See also verses 11 and 16b-17.) GNB omits **O** as archaic, but other languages have common ways of indicating the vocative. **Glorious in power** describes the **right hand** as great or majestic in strength. NAB has "magnificent," and GNB has ***awesome***.

It is important to note the repetition of **Thy right hand, O LORD**. This poetic feature is characteristic of each of the three responses in the song. (See verses 11 and 16b.) GNB unfortunately abandons this pattern. **Shatters the enemy** uses a verb found only here and in Judges 10.8, where RSV gives it the meaning of "crush." GNB has a similar idea: ***it breaks the enemy in pieces***. Here again, the tense of the verb is not indicated, so the translator must interpret the context. NRSV and others have "shattered," but the present tense gives a timeless quality to the poem. (See below at verse 13.) **Enemy** may be understood as singular (the Pharaoh) or as collective (the Egyptians).

II. Yahweh Is Greater Than All the Gods

15.7 **In the greatness of thy majesty thou overthrowest thy adversaries;**
thou sendest forth thy fury, it consumes them like stubble.

In majestic triumph you overthrow your foes;
your anger blazes out and burns them up like straw.

Verses 7-11, the second part of the song, are addressed to Yahweh throughout and speak of his power in more general terms. Muilenburg sees verses 7-8 as another "hymnic confession." **In the greatness of thy majesty** is literally "in the abundance of your height (or loftiness)." GNB has ***In majestic triumph***. Here it may be understood as "Because of your great majesty" or "because you always triumph." **Thou overthrowest thy adversaries** uses a verb meaning to break down or destroy. **Adversaries** is derived from a verb that means to stand up or rise. Here the participle means "those who rise up against you."

Thou sendest forth thy fury uses the verb "to let go," the same word used in the demand to "let my people go." It means to release or give free play to something. Here it is Yahweh's **fury**, or *anger*, which comes from the word "to burn or become hot." It is therefore related to what follows: **it consumes them like stubble**, referring back to the **adversaries** in the first line. So NIV has "You unleashed your burning anger; it consumed them like stubble." **Consumes** is the word "to eat," but here it gives the picture of fire that "devours" the **stubble. Stubble** refers to the dried grain stalks that burn easily. In Exo 5.12 it is distinguished from "straw," but elsewhere it seems to refer to *straw*, or even "chaff" (NJB).

15.8 **At the blast of thy nostrils the waters piled up,**
the floods stood up in a heap;
the deeps congealed in the heart of the sea.

You blew on the sea and the water piled up high;
it stood up straight like a wall;
the deepest part of the sea became solid.

Note that this verse has three lines in parallel. **At the blast of thy nostrils** is literally "by the wind of your nostrils." This figure of speech is an anthropomorphism, meaning that God is described as though he were a human. So this suggests the vivid picture of Yahweh blowing through his nose to divide **the waters** (Exo 14.21). **The waters** is simply the plural form of "water." **Piled up** is a Hebrew word used only here, but the context suggests the meaning of being heaped or dammed up.

The floods comes from the word "to flow." Here it parallels **waters** and **deeps** in lines 1 and 3, so one can say "flowing waters" (NASB) or "surging waves" (TOT). GNB weakens the parallel pattern by using ***it*** for the singular ***water*** in the first line. **Stood up in a heap** is literally "they stood just like a *ned*," but the meaning of *ned* is uncertain. So translations vary: ***wall*** (GNB, NJV, NIV), "bank" (REB), "dyke" (NJB), and "mound" (NAB).

The deeps is the same word translated as "floods" in verse 5. **Congealed** means to thicken or become solid. NJV has "The deeps froze," but this should not be understood literally. Some languages may need to say "they became like frozen," changing the metaphor to a simile. **In the heart of the sea** is literally what the Hebrew says, but NAB says "in the midst of the sea." GNB combines the terms in this line: ***the deepest part of the sea became solid.*** This does not refer to the sea bed but to the ***deepest part*** of the ***water.***

15.9 **The enemy said, 'I will pursue, I will overtake,**
I will divide the spoil, my desire shall have its fill of them.
I will draw my sword, my hand shall devour them.'

The enemy said, 'I will pursue them and catch them;
I will divide their wealth and take all I want;
I will draw my sword and take all they have.'

Verse 9 has three lines in parallel, each with two clauses, and each clause showing successive actions. In rapid staccato style they suggest the over-confident plans in the mind of the **enemy**. Lines 2 and 3 may need to be interchanged for logical sequence. **The enemy** is the same word as in verse 6. **Said**, literally "he said," may introduce the words spoken by the Egyptians (collectively) or by the Pharaoh himself. **I will pursue** has no direct object, so GNB adds ***them,*** meaning the Israelites, even though they are not mentioned until verse 13. **I will overtake** simply means "I will **catch them.**"

I will divide the spoil refers to any goods, animals, or people taken captive by a conquering army and shared with all the men. TOT has "I will share out the plunder." GNB adds the possessive pronoun: ***I will***

divide their wealth. **My desire shall have its fill of them** is literal. The word for **desire** is *nefesh,* which King James Version (KJV) often mistranslates as "soul." Here, however, KJV more correctly has "my lust." Basically the word refers to the throat, suggesting the idea of "desire" (NRSV) or "appetite" (REB). REB has "I shall glut my appetite on them," and NIV has "I will gorge myself on them." Since *nefesh* frequently represents the first person pronoun, GNB changes this to ***I will . . . take all I want,*** with some poetic loss.

I will draw my sword uses the verb meaning to "unsheath" (TOT) or "bare" (NJV) a bladed weapon. The **sword** was probably a long dagger with a straight double-edged blade about 18 inches long. **My hand shall destroy them** uses a verb that means to dispossess, or to separate someone from his property. So NAB has "My hand shall despoil them," and REB has "I shall rid myself of them." This is the basis for GNB's ***I will . . . take all they have,*** which parallels ***I will . . . take all I want.***

15.10 **Thou didst blow with thy wind, the sea covered them;**
they sank as lead in the mighty waters.

But one breath from you, LORD, and the Egyptians were drowned;
they sank like lead in the terrible water.

Thou didst blow with thy wind repeats the idea in verse 8, suggesting that Yahweh blew on **the sea**. The word for **wind** also means ***breath,*** which may be intended here. GNB suggests that it took only ***one breath*** to cause the divided waters to return. NJV removes the "anthropomorphism" (see verse 8) with: "You made your wind blow." GNB adds ***LORD*** for better style, but it is not in the Hebrew. **The sea covered them** uses the same verb as in verse 5. The same word for **sea** is used in verses 1, 4, and 8. **Them**, of course, refers to the Egyptians.

They sank as lead uses a verb found only here, but its meaning is suggested by **lead**, a metal so heavy that it would quickly "sink." This expression echoes verse 5, and in a similar way it introduces the second "response" in the following verse. **In the mighty waters** may be thought of as "terrible waters" (NJB) or "swelling waves" (REB). **Waters** is simply the plural of "water," as in verse 8, but with the adjective, **mighty**, the unruly primeval ocean is meant, as in verse 5.

15.11 **"Who is like thee, O LORD, among the gods?**
Who is like thee, majestic in holiness,
terrible in glorious deeds, doing wonders?

"LORD, who among the gods is like you?
Who is like you, wonderful in holiness?
Who can work miracles and mighty acts like yours?

This verse is a second response of praise to Yahweh and concludes the second strophe. (See verses 6 and 16b-17.) **Who is like thee** is a rhetorical question, meaning "No other god is like you, LORD" (TOT). **O LORD** is vocative, as in verse 6. **Among the gods** refers to other deities as though they existed. The word for **gods** is the plural form of *'el,* used in verse 2 for "my God." The form is *'elim,* not *'elohim.*

Who is like thee repeats the same question for poetic effect. (See the same feature in verses 6 and 16b.) **Majestic in holiness** simply means "for you are majestic and holy" (TOT). **Majestic** is the same word used in verse 6 for "glorious." **Holiness** has the basic meaning of being separate from what is common or profane. Here it is that quality of God that makes him different from humans. The Greek Septuagint has "among the holy ones" instead of **in holiness,** meaning that Yahweh is greater than the other gods. This improves the parallelism with the first line, but most translations stay with the Hebrew.

Terrible in glorious deeds is still part of the second question. **Terrible** is a participle meaning "one who is feared." **In glorious deeds** is one word meaning "in praiseworthy (things)." So REB has "worthy of awe and praise." **Doing wonders,** literally "doer of (the) extraordinary," may be translated as "worker of wonders" (NAB, NJB, REB), or "you perform miracles" (TOT). GNB changes the entire line into another rhetorical question: *Who can work miracles and mighty acts like yours?*

III. Yahweh Will Establish His People

15.12 **Thou didst stretch out thy right hand,**
the earth swallowed them.

You stretched out your right hand,
and the earth swallowed our enemies.

The third confession of faith, according to the threefold pattern, is in verses 12-14. Most translations connect verse 12 with the preceding verses because it still speaks about the deliverance at the sea. But in form it relates more closely to what follows. The very first word, **Thou didst stretch out**, is strikingly similar to the first words in the two lines of verse 13, "Thou didst lead" and "Thou didst guide." There is also a similarity of sound in the Hebrew, *natitha - nachitha - nehalta.* And verse 11, interpreted as a response, serves as a conclusion to the second strophe.

Thou didst stretch out thy right hand echoes the double reference made in verse 6 to Yahweh's **right hand**, which represents his power. **The earth swallowed them** is a bit surprising, for **earth** is used rather than "sea." It may be that the "underworld" (TOT) is referred to here, which would still be the land beneath the sea, as in Jonah 2.6. The word for **swallowed** literally means to gulp down, suggesting swift action and sudden death. This vividly describes how the forces of nature are completely under Yahweh's power.

15.13 **"Thou hast led in thy steadfast love thy people whom thou hast redeemed,**
thou hast guided them by thy strength to thy holy abode.

Faithful to your promise, you led the people you had rescued;
by your strength you guided them to your sacred land.

Thou hast led . . . thy people is past tense in English, but this is not clearly indicated in the Hebrew.[4] In fact, the tense of most of the verbs in verses 13-17 must be handled according to the translators' choice of setting. NIV, for example, uses the future tense, "you *will* lead the people," but this limits the setting to the time when the Israelites were just beginning their journey of faith. NJV, on the other hand, uses the present tense, "In your love You lead the people." This allows for a meaningful expression of faith for future generations. Most translations, however, place this in the past tense. (See the comment at verse 17.)

In thy steadfast love uses the word *chesed,* which means "unfailing love" (NIV), "constant love" (REB), or "faithful love" (TOT). GNB expresses this as ***Faithful to your promise***. **The people whom thou hast redeemed**

refers to the Israelites whom Yahweh has ***rescued*** from the king of Egypt. The word used here for **redeemed** refers to "buying back" family members who had been sold as slaves.

Thou hast guided them (NIV, "you *will* guide them") is a word often used for leading or helping along a person or animal that is handicapped. **By thy strength** is the same word used in verse 2. **To thy holy abode** is literally "to the destination of your holiness," which would be Yahweh's place of residence. It is not clear whether this refers to ***your sacred land,*** or the "mountain" or "sanctuary" mentioned in verse 17. Others have "habitation" (NASB) or "dwelling-place" (REB). It is **holy,** or set apart, because of Yahweh's holiness. (See verse 11.)

15.14 **The peoples have heard, they tremble;**
pangs have seized on the inhabitants of Philistia.

The nations have heard, and they tremble with fear;
the Philistines are seized with terror.

Verses 14-16a give the third narrative account, which most translations place either in the past or present. NIV, however, uses the future tense in order to retain the supposed original setting of the song. These verses then become a prediction, or statement of assurance, about the journey to the promised land which is still to take place.[5]

The peoples have heard refers to groups of people, or ***nations,*** four of which are mentioned by name. It is not stated what they **have heard,** but it obviously refers to the way Yahweh has delivered the Israelites. (NIV's "will hear" suggests that the news has not yet reached these nations.) **They tremble** means to shake in fear, so GNB adds ***they tremble with fear.*** (NRSV has changed this to past tense, "they trembled.")

Pangs is the word for the labor pains of a woman giving birth. A related meaning would be "anguish" (NAB) or "agony" (NJV), but GNB takes this a bit further with ***terror.*** **Have seized** is a descriptive word meaning "laid hold of," or "gripped" (NAB and others). **On the inhabitants of Philistia** refers, of course, to ***the Philistines,*** who lived along the coastal plain in southwest Palestine.[6] **Inhabitants** is literally "sitters," or "dwellers."

15.15 **Now are the chiefs of Edom dismayed;**
the leaders of Moab, trembling seizes them;
all the inhabitants of Canaan have melted away.

The leaders of Edom are terrified;
Moab's mighty men are trembling;
the people of Canaan lose their courage.

Now translates the Hebrew *'oz,* a word that may point to a particular time or emphasize what follows. Some translations using the past tense have "Then" (NEB, NAB, NRSV), while others omit it entirely. Brevard Childs translates it as "Indeed." **The chiefs of Edom** refers to the tribal ***leaders,*** or "princes" (NAB), of a nation to the southeast of Palestine. NJV interprets the word as "clans," which is also possible. **Are . . . dismayed** really means to be ***terrified.***

The leaders of Moab, literally "rams of Moab," refers to "men of power." GNB's ***Moab's mighty men*** uses alliteration to compensate somewhat for the lost metaphor. **Moab** was a nation southeast of Palestine, across the Jordan River. The word for **trembling** is less common than that used in verse 14. NJB has "panic." **Seizes them** is the same word as verse 14.

All the inhabitants of Canaan refers to the Canaanites, but more specifically to the "dwellers" (NAB) of central Palestine. The same word is used in verse 14. **Have melted away** translates a word that also means to waver back and forth, so here it carries the meaning of being disheartened, or losing courage (GNB).

15.16 **Terror and dread fall upon them;**
because of the greatness of thy arm, they are as still as a stone,
till thy people, O LORD, pass by,
till the people pass by whom thou hast purchased.

Terror and dread fall upon them.
They see your strength, O LORD, and stand helpless with fear
until your people have marched past—
the people you set free from slavery.

Terror and **dread** are synonyms in the Hebrew, but the second word also carries the meaning of trembling. **Fall upon them** is a word that suggests falling unintentionally, or unexpectedly. **Them** refers to all the nations mentioned in verses 14 and 15.

Because of the greatness of thy arm is literally "by your great arm." This is an idiom for power or ***strength,*** in the same way that "hand" and "right hand" are used in verses 6 and 12. GNB advances the vocative ***LORD*** from the third to the second line to make it clear that this is addressed to Yahweh. **They are as still as a stone** is the result of Yahweh's powerful **arm**. The word for **still** means to be silent or dumb, not necessarily motionless. But **as a stone** also suggests the idea of not moving, so both ideas may be implied. GNB's ***stand helpless with fear*** tries to express both.

Till thy people . . . pass by refers to the Israelites passing through the territory of the four nations just mentioned. The vocative **O LORD** again marks the third response of praise, which here extends into verse 17. Following the pattern of the responses in verses 6 and 11, this phrase is repeated for poetic effect, with the addition of **the people . . . whom thou hast purchased**. The word here usually means to buy or acquire, so NRSV has "acquired." In some places, however, the same word means to produce or create, so Muilenburg translates, "whom thou hast created." GNB tries to catch both meanings, ***the people you set free from slavery.***

15.17 **Thou wilt bring them in, and plant them on thy own mountain,**
the place, O LORD, which thou hast made for thy abode,
the sanctuary, O LORD, which thy hands have established.

You bring them in and plant them on your mountain,
the place that you, LORD, have chosen for your home,
the Temple that you yourself have built.

This verse is an extension of the response beginning at verse 16b. Here the question of tense becomes crucial. **Thou wilt bring them in** is literally "you will cause them to enter." Most translations shift to the future tense with this verse, giving the song the historic setting of the

Exodus, *before* the entrance into the promised land. A few, however (NEB, NAB, NRSV), retain the past tense ("You brought them in"), giving it the cultic setting of the worshiping community *after* the people were settled in Canaan. GNB's use of the present tense (***You bring them in***) is certainly legitimate, and it gives the song a timeless quality that allows the worshipers to celebrate both past deliverance and future hope.

And plant them uses the term for planting a garden, meaning that Yahweh will establish them in their new location. **On thy own mountain,** literally "on the mountain of your heritage," identifies it as an inherited possession. In time it came to refer to Mount Zion in Jerusalem, which was later recognized as Yahweh's **abode**. (See verse 13.) **The place, O LORD, which thou hast made for thy abode** is literally "a place for you to sit, you made (it), Yahweh." GNB is more natural, ***the place that you, LORD, have chosen for your home***.

The word for **sanctuary** is literally "a holy place." Later generations identified this with ***the Temple*** in Jerusalem, which of course was not built until the time of Solomon, some three hundred years after the time of Moses. **Which thy hands have established** uses a verb meaning to prepare or make firm. So GNB has, ***the Temple that you yourself have built***. **O LORD** occurs twice as a vocative, but this second instance is really *'adonay* ("O Lord") in the Masoretic Text. Most translations follow the Greek Septuagint and other ancient Hebrew texts, which read it as Yahweh.

Closing Doxology

15.18 **The LORD will reign for ever and ever."**

You, LORD, will be king forever and ever."

This is the "closing doxology" of the song. It refers to Yahweh as a king who **will reign for ever and ever**. **LORD** is referred to in the third person, but GNB changes the verb to second person. The verb literally means to rule as king or to ***be king***. **For ever and ever** is literally "for all time and continuing."

Concluding Comments

The song itself concludes with verse 18, but verses 19-21 place it again within the intended historical setting of the Exodus story. Just as verse 1a had introduced the song in the context of Yahweh's miraculous deliverance of his people at the sea, so these verses bring the worshiping community back to the stark reality with which chapter 14 had ended. The Israelites now find themselves on the other side of the sea, with Egyptian slavery behind them and a new beginning ahead of them.

The following chapters, beginning immediately with 15.22 and continuing to 19.1, give a preview of the difficulties the people were to face in the wilderness. They proved to be a time of testing, and the relationship between Moses and that motley crowd of ex-slaves had to be worked out. But this particular moment was a time for celebration and rejoicing. So Miriam, "the sister of Aaron," who is also called "the prophetess," picks up the opening words of Moses' song and leads all the women in singing and dancing. The only change in the words of 1b is in the first word—"I (Moses) will sing" now becomes "(You all) sing"! And succeeding generations have continued to sing of Yahweh's marvelous deliverance of his people through all generations to the present day.

Moses' Song at the Sea became the most powerful expression of the core of Israel's faith for the worshiping community. It's theme is central to the entire Hebrew scriptures. It permeates the story of the Exodus with the message that God's grace is always the basis of God's law. In this way, the book of Exodus should be considered as "the Gospel of the Old Testament."

Notes

[1] Scholars are not in agreement as to either the date or the unity of this song. Martin Noth (1962, p.123) considers it to be "a relatively late piece," which in its present form "is no longer a unity." On the other hand, Nahum Sarna (1991, p.75) believes it may well be "the oldest piece of sustained poetry in the Hebrew Bible." And Philip Hyatt (1971, p.163) observes that "It is vivid, is carefully composed by strophes, and makes excellent use of assonance, repetition, and climax." Brevard Childs (1974, p.244) concludes that "the Song does not reflect any one genre in its form

which would give the key to its function within the early life of the nation."

[2] See his "A Liturgy on the Triumphs of Yahweh" in Studia Biblica et Semitica, T. C. Vriezen Dedicata (Wageningen, H. Veenman & Zonen, 1966), pp.238-50. The adaptations made here include providing titles for the three main divisions, counting verse 14 as narrative rather than confession, and considering verse 17 as an extension of the response in 16b.

[3] These are the printing features followed in the Handbook series, published by the United Bible Societies. Other translations quoted are identified in each instance. (See the list of abbreviations.)

[4] Hebrew verb forms show the action as completed or incomplete, but they do not clearly show whether the action takes place in the past, present, or future. This has to be determined by the syntax and/or the total context. In Hebrew poetry, which tends to use fewer words in a brevity of style, the syntax is less structured and a time context less definitive.

[5] A comparison of 12 leading English translations reveals the different views of the translators regarding the most appropriate setting for this song within the worshiping community. For example, the time context envisioned for verses 13-16, and for verse 17, may be summarized as follows,

	Verses 13-16	**Verse 17**
Past:	NEB, REB, NRSV, NAB	NEB, NRSV, NAB
Present:	RSV, GNB, NJV, NJB, JB	GNB
Future:	NIV, KJV (NASB)	(the others)

[6] Historians believe it is unlikely that the Philistines had already settled in Palestine when the Israelites left Egypt. These war-like people originally came from the area of the Aegean Sea in the early twelfth century B.C. For this reason, scholars insist that this song could not have been written until after that time. This, however, should not in any way affect the translation.

References

Childs, Brevard S., *The Book of Exodus, A Critical, Theological Commentary* (The Old Testament Library). Philadelphia, Westminster Press, 1974.

Durham, John I., *Exodus* (Word Biblical Commentary). Waco, Texas, Word Books, 1987.

Hyatt, J. Philip., *Exodus* (New Century Bible). London, Oliphants, 1971.

Muilenburg, James, "A Liturgy on the Triumphs of Yahweh." In *Studia Biblica et Semitica, T. C. Vriezen Dedicata,* pp.238-50. Wageningen, H. Veenman & Zonen, 1966.

Noth, Martin, *Exodus, A Commentary* (Old Testament Library). Translated by J. S. Bowden. Philadelphia, Westminster Press, 1962.

Sarna, Nahum, *Exodus* (New Torah Commentary). Philadelphia, Jewish Publication Society of America, 1991.

Index

Index of Scripture References